TODD FULTZ

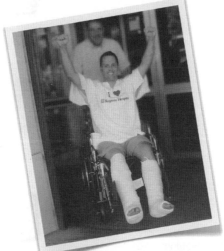

THE YEAR OF
LITTLE
VICTORIES

S0-DMY-664

VICTORY
PRESS

Copyright ©2010 by Todd Fultz
All rights reserved.
No portion of this book may be reproduced—mechanically, electronically, or by any
other means, including photocopying—without written permission of the publisher.

The Year of Little Victories / by Todd Fultz

ISBN: 978-0-9831311-0-6 (Hardcover — Limited First Edition) _____ / 365
Printed November 10, 2010

ISBN: 978-0-9831311-1-3 (Paperback Edition)

Cover & Interior: Lookout Design, Inc.
Printed by Bayport Printing House, Inc., Bayport, Minnesota

Victory Press, LLC
4730 Neal Avenue North
Stillwater, MN 55082

10 11 12 13 14 15   (BPH)   10 9 8 7 6 5 4 3 2

IN MEMORIAM

*From the time of the accident until the publication
of this book, we lost some very dear friends.
Their lives were marked by extraordinary love and compassion,
and my life is richer
for having known them.*

Dave Doyscher

Doug Swenson

Jill Roiger-Hines

Debby Petersen

Benjamin Ngede

Pat Grant

Bob Beattie

Keith Olson

DEDICATION

This book is dedicated to
the many people who prayed for me,
who sent me letters,
who stopped and visited,
who cared for my family,
who helped with my business.
This book is for those of you
who encouraged, loved, and shared your
time with me during my recovery.

This book is dedicated to you.

EDITOR'S NOTE:

This book is a personal and intimate look at an event that united a family and a community. The foundation of this book is the CaringBridge site that was the Fultz family's main line of communication in the year following the accident.

In each entry the day is identified, starting with the day of the accident as Day One. There were no CaringBridge entries for the first two days: those days are a composite of the recollections of those swept into the aftermath of this horrific accident.

Beginning with Day Three, we had Todd go back and reread the CaringBridge entries and narrate his true thoughts at the time. With sufficient distance from the tragedy and the recovery, he was able to recall and be transparent about the scope of the emotions and experiences contained in each day.

Guestbook entries on CaringBridge were a major source of support to Todd and his family, and we have included many of them in the book, and more in a special section at the conclusion of the book. Everyone who signed the CaringBridge site has been included. Reading the entries gives the true sense of community that enveloped the Fultz family in its warm embrace as they went through this year of incredible uncertainty.

It is our hope that what you read here will bring you courage and inspiration in the events of your day-to-day life. We hope you'll find strength for the hard times, and a reminder to rejoice in the simple blessings of family and friends.

We hope you will learn to work for, and to gain, your own little victories.

Adam Swenson
Roseville, Minnesota
October 2010

DAY 1

TODD:

I lingered for just a moment before I left, watching my wife paint the spindles on our front porch. When I tapped her on the shoulder, she stood and turned to face me. I gave her a quick kiss and told her I'd be back soon: I was just making a quick run up the road to check on a job site. She said, "I'll see you later" and returned to her painting.

I climbed into my black Oldsmobile sedan, started the engine, and pulled out onto the road. My sales associate, Elliot, followed behind me in his truck. I glanced into my rearview mirror now and then to check on his truck as we crawled down the quiet streets of Stillwater's North Hill, past tall oak trees and houses with fences that gave way to fields and open spaces.

When we came to Manning Avenue I turned north, joining the other cars driving on that sunny June afternoon. I remember feeling quite content as I cruised along at sixty miles an hour down the serene country road. All was right in my world.

A dump truck lumbered toward me in the oncoming lane, then a red car appeared out of nowhere as the driver pulled over to pass the dump truck. **Bam!**

Since both cars were going sixty, the collision speed was 120 miles per hour—it was both impossibly fast and unimaginably violent. I blacked out. I learned later that the impact caused my car to go airborne, spiraling through the air like a football. I owe my life to the fact that the car landed on its wheels. Had it landed roof down, it would have resulted in massive head trauma and broken my neck.

Seconds later I awoke. Everything around me was grotesquely twisted and crushed. My airbag was deployed, the steering wheel was in my lap. The engine compartment was smoldering a foot in front of me, and an incredible feeling of claustrophobia set it.

I couldn't feel my legs, and I was pinned in by the steering wheel and the dash. Toxic smoke filled my nose with the acrid smell of burning metal, rubber, oil, and brake fluid. I felt a gurgling sensation in my lungs, like I was drowning slowly from the inside. My back was in searing pain, as though someone had stood me up with my hands outstretched then hit me repeatedly with a sledgehammer.

Since both cars were going sixty, the collision speed was 120 miles per hour—it was both impossibly fast and unimaginably violent.

I didn't want to die like this, and that meant I had to get myself out. There was no time to wait for the first responders. Elliot arrived outside my car, but was visibly cautious as he approached.

I stretched my arms out behind me and grabbed the backs of the headrests, and pulled as hard as I could. My legs didn't work and would only come with me as deadweight: that much was abundantly clear.

After wrestling my body out of the driver's seat I was sitting on the armrest between the seats. I wriggled and wrestled some more and slithered my way into the back seat.

From there I dragged my body to the only opening, a broken window in the rear driver's side door. I reached my hands out the window to the door frame and began to pull, trying to extricate myself. Then the strong hands of Elliot and Mr. Nash, an off-duty first responder who happened to be driving by just after the accident occurred, pulled me out. They carried me twenty feet away from the crash and laid me flat on my back in the road, waiting for help to arrive.

It felt surreal, lying on the pavement with that center line inches away, watching the scene unfold. Elliot and Mr. Nash were both on the phone with 911, and I lay there helpless in excruciating pain, lungs filling with fluid, my nose full of the scent of burning Oldsmobile.

Above me the sun shone down. The sounds of sirens pierced through the screams of pain and shouted instructions.

Seven minutes had elapsed since I kissed my wife goodbye.

ELLIOT:

My eyes settled on his taillights as we drove north on Manning.

An oncoming red car veered over. There was no time. I knew they were going to hit.

I jerked my own steering wheel to the right and slammed on the brakes to miss the sudden obstacles in the roadway. My truck slid into the ditch, hitting a tree and a fencepost before it came to a stop. My heart pounded rapid fire like a machine gun inside my chest as I flung my door open. I ran to Todd's car, waving for help to come. I feared what I'd find there.

Could he have survived that?

The little black car that held my friend, mentor, and coworker was crushed, utterly destroyed, the front bumper pushed back nearly to the steering wheel. Flames leapt out of the engine compartment and my mind filled with the thousands of exploding cars I've seen in television and movies.

Todd was conscious but confused. I called out to him, telling him it was going to be okay, just hold on.

Incredibly, through the smoke and broken glass I saw him start to maneuver his body in an effort to escape the deadly confines.

Thick noxious smoke blew into my face and stung my eyes. I worried about how much time we had to get Todd out from that burning piece of scrap metal. Then a man named Mr. Nash showed up beside me. We tried to open the door to pull him out, but it wasn't going to happen. As soon as it was possible we pulled Todd out the rear driver's side window as gently as we could, given the circumstances. We carried him twenty feet, and laid him on the ground.

I called 911. Cars were beginning to back up on the road now. A man driving a pickup fetched a fire extinguisher and put out Todd's car. Flashing lights and sirens signaled the arrival of several police cars and ambulances.

I'd really never known trauma or hardship up to that point in my life, so the experience of seeing such a life-or-death situation was that much more jarring. Though I dreaded it with every fiber of my being, I knew what I had to do next.

I looked over as the first responders were cutting off Todd's clothes, down to his boxers. He lay flat on his back on the pavement, blood everywhere. He screamed in pain as they poked him, trying to determine the extent of his injuries.

With a heavy heart, I flipped open my phone and called Erica.

ERICA:

The phone rang incessantly. Annoyed by it, I put down my paintbrush and went inside to take the call. On the other end of the line was Elliot's voice. "Todd has been in a little accident."

"Is it really bad?" I asked.

"No," Elliot said. "He's doing OK."

I threw down the phone and ran to my car.

As I sped toward Manning Avenue I was conscious of the ambulance sounds rising, but that did not prepare me. What I saw there made my heart stop.

There were more spinning red and blue lights than I have ever seen in my life—the emergency vehicles formed a barricade across the road—and somewhere in the middle of this chaos lay my husband. I pulled my car over, jumped out, and sprinted.

My nose filled with the smell of burning rubber and metal. The sight of Todd's demolished car took my breath away. The front end was folded in on itself like an accordion. Todd was lying on the ground, his clothes cut away, with EMTs hovering above him. One of the EMTs called out, "Don't let her over here."

Elliot tried to hold me back, but I got past him. Desperate, I ran to Todd, crying and calling out for help, though help was already there.

Todd said, "Erica, calm down. I'm the one who was in the accident."

Once I'd had a moment to think, I asked Elliot to dig through Todd's car to find his wallet and cell phone. In the background I heard a voice whispering to someone nearby: "That guy's not going to make it." He was talking about Todd.

I looked over and saw Ron, the driver who had hit Todd. His injuries were massive: I thought he was dead.

The EMTs loaded Todd into an ambulance en route to Regions Hospital. I climbed into the front seat to be with him for the trip. Riding inside that ambulance was immensely frustrating, as cars along the highways failed to move over fast enough. My body was taken over by pure adrenaline.

When we arrived at the hospital, Todd was wheeled off into the ER. Before he left, I told him that I loved him. Inconsolable and pacing in the waiting room, I waited for Todd's parents to arrive.

Elliot arrived first, about twenty minutes after the ambulance. Though he was young and didn't have much experience with crisis, he was a very strong and calming presence for me as I waited for news I knew wouldn't be good.

EUNICE FULTZ:

When I got the phone call from Erica, I didn't recognize her voice. She cried into the phone that there had been an accident. Todd was going to the hospital.

Neither I nor Don knew a thing about the accident. We didn't know what Todd's condition was. Nothing.

Everything was a blur from there. We made sure Todd and Erica's three kids were picked up from school and daycare. They would be looked after by our daughter, Tami. We were numb as we climbed into the car and drove straight to Regions.

We had no idea what awaited us.

DON FULTZ:

I was at the Twins game with my son-in-law, Chuck, and grandson, Shawn. The game was in the eighth inning—we agreed it was time to leave and get a head start on the crowd exiting the Metrodome.

Chuck's cell phone rang and he answered. It was hard to hear because of the crowd, but soon Chuck said, "We have to leave right now. Todd has been in an accident and may have a broken leg."

Tami had dropped us off at the stadium and she was waiting for us in the spot we'd agreed on.

We did not have a lot to go on, but decided to head for our townhouse in Shoreview. When Eunice returned with the kids, Chuck and Tami insisted that they would stay with all five of the children so that Eunice and I could head for the hospital.

It was a quiet ride to Regions, with Eunice recapping what little she knew about the accident and Todd's physical condition (beyond the possible broken leg).

Driving to the hospital, parking, and getting to the emergency waiting room seemed like an eternity. When we got there, most of the family and friends were already present. Erica was really the first to speak with us—at that point she was remarkably calm and lucid. She explained more about the accident and the extent of the injuries based upon what she knew at that point. We visited briefly and quietly with the other family and friends huddled together near the end of the waiting room. We began to hear words like "Todd is very fortunate to be alive" and "We think he is going to be fine, but things are a lot more serious than any of us realized."

Someone in the group suggested a prayer, and that I should lead. We all joined hands, forming a circle. I remember asking God for a miracle of healing, expressing gratefulness for the medical team that was attending Todd in those very moments, and commending Todd into the good hands of Jesus.

Some official person from the hospital asked if Eunice and I and Erica would join her in a conference room. It was then that we understood the reality of the extent of the injuries. Todd was going to be taken into surgery to inspect his internal organs for damage. It was at that same time that Todd was being wheeled on a cart outside the door of our conference room. We had a chance to visit with him quickly, tell him we love him, and assure him that the doctors were going to do whatever was needed to get him into a stable condition.

That was around 6:00 p.m. The initial surgery lasted until 11:30 when the doctor came out to explain his findings. There were a number of very serious injuries to Todd's ankles, legs, pelvis, and lower back. There was perhaps a laceration of the liver, otherwise it appeared that all the internal organs were in good shape. The doctor indicated that Todd's age and positive attitude—yes, the medical team was already aware of it—were highly in his favor. He said that if this had happened to a much older person they might not even proceed much farther, but that Todd had a very good chance at a good (but long) recovery.

Around midnight we decided to head home: Todd would be in the critical care unit and there was no point in waiting around much longer. We were so very grateful for Tami's willingness to make sure the children were cared for so we could be at the hospital. It was a most wonderful gift that Tami gave to us all.

JUDITH SAVAGE:

I had just finished a session with one of my therapy patients when Erica called. She said that Todd had been in an accident, that she was leaving now, and to come quick: it was serious.

I immediately called the rest of my patients for the day, telling them we'd have to reschedule. Assuming he'd be in the Stillwater hospital, I drove as fast as I could through rush hour to get there. The staff kindly informed me that they had no one by that name, then said he was likely at Regions. After they confirmed this through a quick phone call, I got back in my car and drove back to St. Paul—what could have been a five minute trip turned into a ninety minute wild goose chase.

Only Erica and Elliot were there when I arrived at Regions. Erica looked stunned and terrified (as I'm sure we all did), but still managed to be an incredibly loyal and strong holding point. She was like a rotational center of gravity that kept everything moving. Her ability to do that under incredible strain was quite impressive.

Elliot was calm, but he had a traumatic look in his eye. As a mental health professional, I'm quite familiar with this state of mind: he had seen very difficult things, had made difficult choices, and had very nearly been in the accident himself. I tried to get him to talk, both to help him and to try to find out any more details that I could.

Todd was in another world on the other side of those doors. The impulse to see him was so strong, but of course we couldn't. All we could do was to wait and try to manage these huge emotions enveloping us.

Nixon showed up and his family came later. Their gentle and genuine presence was comforting. While we were all in the midst of incredible heartache and uncertainty, their quiet presence was lovely.

ARAM DESTEIAN:

I got the call at 5:00 that Todd, my half brother, had been in a car accident. My mother, Judith, (Todd's birth mother) had gone to the Stillwater hospital after getting news of the crash, only to find out that Todd had been taken to Regions in St. Paul.

I wondered then why Todd was at Regions, since it's much further away, and it dawned on me: Regions has a Level 1 Trauma Center. Maybe this wasn't such a little accident after all.

My girlfriend and I had carpooled to work, and I had to wait for her to pick me up. We ran into traffic the whole way there, and I was beside myself. When we arrived in the hospital we ran up to the waiting room, and I found a small group of people there hoping, praying, and waiting for news. Erica was there along with Todd's parents, Don and Eunice. Judith was also there along with Elliot and one of Todd's workers named Nixon.

Everyone expect Elliot was huddled together in a sort of survival instinct: there was an incredible feeling of solidarity. Elliot was pacing the floor, making and receiving calls on Todd's cell phone, keeping the business affairs in order.

My mom, Judith, is a psychologist. I have never before seen her so pale and frightened.

Todd's father, Don, was a longtime minister and he was the only one who seemed to be holding it together. Elliot handled it by staying on the phone, talking business to keep his mind off all the large and impossible questions, the things that were heavy in the air but that we didn't talk about.

We prayed a lot, Don saw to that.

Around 7:30 the doctor came out and told us the extent of Todd's injuries. They were operating and had worked through all the internal organs and had Todd stabilized. The operation, however, would continue into the very early morning.

The doctor had catalogued Todd's injuries. As he read off the checklist it seemed like it was four pages long: a fracture of his pelvis, an open fracture in his right leg, his right ankle was shot, and on from there.

At 8:00 we ate even though we didn't feel like it, and people started leaving around 10:00. I knew I had to stay: I wouldn't get any sleep at home anyway.

Don and Eunice left around midnight after the doctor came out with a further report. After hearing that they felt safe to leave.

Though it was 12:30, it didn't feel late yet. All the lights were on, medical staff were coming and going, and people were waiting anxiously for news about their loved ones. It's much like a casino: once you step inside those doors, all connections with the world outside are severed and a new artificial, always-on reality is created.

Erica and I were the only two left after midnight. We just sat quietly, as there was nothing to say. Todd was still in surgery and had been for ten hours. The lights went off and came back on. We tried to sleep, but sleep wouldn't come.

I thought back on my own knee surgery, remembering that it lasted two hours. *There can't be more than five knee surgeries worth of stuff to do*, I thought.

My mind circled around and around, running various contingency trees and what-if scenarios. I tried to boil things down, to simplify them. What if Todd can't walk? OK, they can get an apartment in Stillwater.

But even as I came up with these, deep down I knew that nothing would be simple. I knew that every question I asked prompted two more, leading me down into an impenetrable tangle.

We sat bone-tired under the ever-present fluorescent lights and waited for news.

DAY 2

ERICA:

As I waited to go back to see him, day one stretched into day two. I heard one nurse say to another, "I can't believe he survived it. Most people bleed out from this."

At 1:30 in the morning we were the only people in the waiting room, and someone came out to get us. They told us Todd was out of surgery and we could come back now. Aram couldn't handle going in yet, so I went it alone.

I had seen Todd before he went into surgery. He looked like himself then: battered, bruised, bloodied, but he was in there. We said I love you to each other.

I had to walk down a long hallway to get to him. Todd was in the last room. As we walked by, each room was filled with a 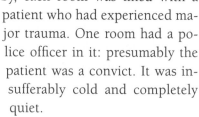 patient who had experienced major trauma. One room had a police officer in it: presumably the patient was a convict. It was insufferably cold and completely quiet.

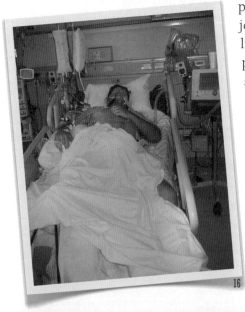

When I slid the door open and stepped into the room, I saw a different Todd. He was intubated and in a medically-induced coma. He had a long incision from surgery and external fixators that made him look like a giant doll that had been melded with an Erector set by a boy with a cruel imagination.

The room was freezing cold. It felt more like a morgue than a recovery room.

I stayed until I couldn't take it anymore and walked back down the long hallway to wait.

Aram came back with me at 4:30 in the morning. When we arrived at the room, we slid the door open, but Aram couldn't make himself enter. He looked at Todd and that one look was enough.

We went back out to the waiting room and fell asleep once the exhaustion caught up with us. Our sleep was punctuated by sirens and announcements over the loudspeakers. We'd only slept twenty minutes or so when a security guard woke us and told us we had to move.

Out the windows we could see the entrance to the emergency room, and a trickle of wounded arriving on foot or by stretcher. Though the world at large was going on, oblivious to the hell we were in the middle of, the influx of ER patients reminded us that there were others going through it too.

> When I slid the door open and stepped into the room, I saw a different Todd. He was intubated and in a medically-induced coma. He had a long incision from surgery and external fixators that made him look like a giant doll that had been melded with an Erector set by a boy with a cruel imagination.

Around 6:30 in the morning we moved to a side room, and then we learned that the family across the hall was Ron's family, the man who had hit Todd. Todd's mother, Eunice, had worked with Ron's wife, Dee, a long time ago and so we had a tenuous connection before this very large and traumatic connection.

We learned then that Ron had been airlifted to Regions. Our feelings were still pretty raw at that point, so we tried to avoid that family.

The problem, however, was that Dee was very nice to us and very concerned with our wellbeing. We were angry at Ron (understandably) but Dee's sweet, calming presence made the emotional situation much more complex.

She was always handing out treats from a cooler, and when Aram fell asleep in the morning, Dee put a blanket on him.

At 10:00 we staked out our own space, putting a sign on the door of one of the smaller waiting rooms that read simply "Fultz."

Todd's friends from college began to show up to check on him, and Aram answered his phone to address the never-ending stream of questions.

By that evening it would become a matter of *when* Todd would recover. He had passed the first big hurtle. He would live.

I went home and collapsed.

.

DAY 3

SATURDAY, JUNE 7, 2008

ERICA: 12:15 PM

Wonderful news! They removed Todd's ventilator just now. He is breathing fine, but quickly. The doctors want that to slow down, but you know Todd: he is anxious. He looks good today: his eyes are clearer, and his swelling has gone down.

With the ventilator out, he is talking a little bit. He is in major pain, so they are treating that with some good pain meds. The surgery for his pelvis is tentatively scheduled for Wednesday. I am going to leave him be a little bit. I just want him to get into his zone. Thanks again for all the well wishes. We are so lucky to be loved by all of you!

ERICA: 3:46 PM

The doctors needed to put a BiPAP (a mask that forces air in) on Todd to help him breathe. With his injury, he isn't able to sit up, and this is causing pressure on the lungs. He can breathe on his own—it's his positioning that they are concerned about. They are hoping the BiPAP will be sufficient. If not, they will have to put the ventilator back in. One step at a time.

He is still in a great deal of pain, he is able to communicate that. He is now going to be able to press the pain drip himself, which will help.

Prayers, prayers, prayers: that's all we can do at this time.

EUNICE AND DON FULTZ: 4:10 PM

Todd and Erica,

This is day number two since the accident and we are pleased to hear that the ventilator has been turned off. This will be a different feel and obviously some strange things can happen until the body responds to that change. It is such a blessing that you are doing so well, even though the drugs probably do not allow you to comprehend everything. Just know that many people are praying for your recovery and rejoicing in the miracle that you are still counted among the living. We thank God for that blessing.

We pray that God will continue to give you strength and perseverance to hang in there and let the body do its healing work along with the great and masterful hands that surround you with their skills.

Love to you and Erica. The children are doing just fine but they miss their daddy. But they know you are doing quite well and they are happy about that.

GUESTBOOK:

Todd and family,

Sorry your family has such a long road ahead of you, but your fight and strength will get you on the road to recovery. Soon you'll be out playing ball with the kids, teaching them how you broke all the records at St. John's on that football field! Take care and God bless.

We will keep you in our prayers! We love the website for updates!

Stacy Iverson

———

Hi Todd, Erica, and kids,

We are thinking of you so often and praying for Todd. What a miracle that he survived such a horrific accident. It sounds like he is making very good progress. We'll keep up the prayers!

We love you,

The Meyers

LOOKING BACK...

I woke up in the ICU. It was quiet. Machines in the room hummed softly to the rhythm of my breathing as I came to terms with this new reality.

There was a tube down my throat. Pain.

I felt like I was going to be sick. My nurse checked on me often—her presence was calming. Erica came and went in a flurry of soft words. It was hard to talk and I was frustrated that she could not stay long.

I remember focusing on the following day, hoping I would be more awake next time I opened my eyes.

DAY 4

SUNDAY, JUNE 8, 2008

ERICA: 11:05 AM

Today is Sunday—one more day down. I slept at the hospital again last night just to make sure everything was OK with his breathing. The doctors put the BiPAP mask back on from midnight to 8:00 am, and he did very well. I went in at 8:00 to see him and they took the mask off for a while.

Just like Todd, he went in to work mode, asking about all the things that needed to be done for tomorrow. It is just amazing to me. I said, "Don't worry, I have it all covered!" I am so happy about his progress.

He is in major pain, and cannot get comfortable—the nurses just keep adjusting his position. I feel so awful, I just wish I could take it away from him. The surgery on Wednesday should help because then he will be able to be in a different angle.

Thank you again for all your prayers, keep them coming. They are being answered!

Love to you all,
Erica

GUESTBOOK:

Todd and family,

I was sitting in church this morning in Lakeville, and a prayer was requested for one of our member's nephews, Todd Fultz. I haven't seen or talked to Todd recently, though I hear his name come up now and again.

Hearing about his accident really hit home. My brother and I played basketball against Todd in high school (I went to Mounds View, class of '87, and my brother Dan to Irondale, class of '86). Both of us think so much of Todd and are pulling for you guys. I will be checking for updates! My heart and prayers goes out to you and your family.

Andy Schultz

———

Dear Erica and Todd, Mary, Tim, and Madeline,

We are grateful for the miracle of life. Know that we love you and are praying that healing and good health return. Todd, you have that fighting spirit, or should we say that winning spirit. Either way, you want to come out on top!

You are on the journey to recovery. We are cheering for all the signs that show progress. Go! Go! Remember, I still have that cheering spirit within me, though I hope I am a little quieter about my yells.

We love you very much and are so proud of you and your family. You are a blessing to so many people.

Love, Mom and Dad Fultz

———

Fultzie,

Only you will understand this one. When things don't seem to be working, just throw the freakin' bomb! Promise all your friends and family that you will keep moving forward down the field and we will get you the ball.

Go deep #2!

Tom Ramboldt

LOOKING BACK...

Focusing on recovery was hard. I told myself to remain calm, willing my muscles to relax. My legs were wrapped like a mummy. I stared at these new pins and rods that were holding my legs together. My back and my pelvis were in constant searing pain.

I thought about the next big surgery. I wanted to get it over with.

DAY 5

MONDAY, JUNE 9, 2008

ERICA: 12:15 PM

I got to the hospital today at about 10:00 am. It was nice to be able to sleep at home with the kids last night. I know they needed me home. Mimi told me that they are just pretending that daddy is on vacation someplace fun. She is such a smart cookie.

Timmy came and laid in bed with me at about 5:00 am and rubbed my head and gave me kisses on my hand. He is taking over, being the little man of the house.

I went to see Todd and he is pretty sleepy. The doctors were able to give him something stronger to control the pain. They also were giving him a drug to try and control blood clots. It seems to be a go for surgery on Wednesday. His hemoglobin has leveled out, so that is a good sign. I think we will see some major improvements after surgery.

Other than that, his face looks good and his eyes are bright. He is in that fighting, determined spirit, so I'm just cheering him on.

Thank you for everyone who has stopped by the hospital. We really appreciate all the visitors. Todd can't have any visitors right now, however. He will be in here for a very long while, so there will be plenty of time to see him in a couple of weeks. Keep that in mind.

In the meantime, keep the prayers coming. We are on the right path. Love to you all!

GUESTBOOK:

We were so shocked to hear about Todd's accident. It is in crisis like this that you find inner strength you never knew you had. It will carry you both through the next several weeks and months. We have your family in our thoughts and prayers and would love to help in any way we can.

Bobby & Jenny Tuccitto

———

Dear Todd and Erica,

We can't tell you how much we are praying for Todd's continued recovery and for strength for your whole family. Both of you and your kids are so special to so many people. Please know that we care deeply and will continue to pray for all of you.

God's blessings,

Amy Karlstad

———

Todd,

First, it is a great relief to hear you are OK and have already started down a path to recovery. It is a story like this that makes us all hug our families a little tighter. If there was anyone strong enough to fight this battle, my money is on you. Know that my family and the greater Ranger/Pony community have you and your family in our thoughts and prayers.

That being said, it just isn't right to have the Forest Lake legend on the injured reserve. So pal, let's get busy and start healing. There are few hundred of us Ranger alums who are a little out of sorts trying to grasp the notion that anyone short of Jack Tatum could slow down the shifty and speedy #2. Back in the day, you were the man that we little junior high punks all aspired to be like: an invincible touchdown machine. Some may call this hero worship, others a mancrush. Whatever: just keep fighting so that we can be inspired by you once again.

With all sincerity, please don't hesitate to ask for help. At a minimum, young Tim and I should have a little chat about how to lull the corner on a 60 Blast Blue.

God be with you and your family.

Andy McCurdy

LOOKING BACK...

Erica went home to be with the kids the night before. They needed her more than I did. Of course I wanted my wife with me, but I knew that the kids would want Mom to hold them and talk with them.

It must be scary for a kid to not have one of your parents around. Imagine the phone ringing off the hook as everyone calls wanting details about the accident.

DAY 6

ERICA: 11:38 AM

More of the same today! Todd had a wonderful nurse last night: she brought the phone into his room so he was able to say goodnight to the kids. Mimi asked why he was talking so funny, and I said that the doctors are giving some very good medicine that makes him talk funny. She got a kick out of it.

The nurses said that he was pretty anxious through the night. I think that his brain is starting to process some things now and you know Todd, he is not one to sit still. All of his levels are stable and they are preparing for surgery tomorrow. It will be a very long one.

The orthopedic surgeon and the neurosurgeon will be working on his pelvis and spine. I think after tomorrow we will start to see some huge differences. In fact, the social worker told me Todd may be moved out of the ICU by this weekend if all goes well! Keep those prayers comin', they are working miracles. The nurse reiterated to me last night how much of a miracle Todd is to be here with us right now!

All my love,
Erica

ERICA: 10:46 PM

Hello everyone! I am sitting here reading everyone's greetings, and it's a testament to how Todd lives his life. He has talked many times to me—and I am sure most of you—about "life without regrets," and I am seeing it at work right now. It is such a blessing to have each of you write in. I ask that all of you channel all of your love and prayers toward Todd at 7:30 tomorrow morning as the surgeons prepare to mend him. The surgery is ten hours, in which they will work on his pelvis, L5, and lumbar system. The neurosurgeon is renowned for the technique he uses in these injuries. Leave it to Todd to get the best! I will update everyone with the progress throughout the day. Thank you all so much!

Love,

Erica

GUESTBOOK:

Todd,

Boyle just told us of your accident and sent us this link. I'm just glad that I'm able to write you an e-mail and you're able to read it. We wish you and your family the best in your recovery. I'd try a little Boyle humor here, but I imagine that laughing is a little painful. Take care and good luck. The amount of people that sign your guestbook is a great reflection of how many people you positively impact!

Tom and Myra Reuter

———

Hi Todd and family,

We just wanted to say hi and to let you and your family know that you are in our thoughts and prayers. We are continuing to pray for physical, spiritual, and emotional healing from this horrible happening. While it may not seem like it right now, it is important to know that God is still on his throne, and he does have a wonderful plan, although we may not see it now.

Blessings and healing,

Kurt and Ann Gramith

LOOKING BACK...

After being in the ICU for nearly a week, I was starting to get familiar with my surroundings and the hospital staff. They were feeding me ice chips, but what I really wanted was water. My mouth and throat were dry, however, and these ice chips were refreshing.

I would be going into surgery on Wednesday morning. I was so scared—people die in surgery.

I would be going into surgery on Wednesday morning. I was so scared—people die in surgery. What if something went wrong? I thought about my family a lot that Tuesday night. I considered what my body had just gone through, and the prospect of a ten-hour surgery to repair the damage that had been done.

Frankly I was overwhelmed. I prayed that the doctor was sleeping well that night and that he would be on his game in the morning.

Ten hours in surgery. Ten hours of mystery.

DAY 7

WEDNESDAY, JUNE 11, 2008

DON: 10:35 AM

Today, June 11, Todd's dad will be writing the update. We arrived at the hospital at 6:40 am and they had already moved Todd to the surgical prep space. He was alert and anxious for the surgical crew to get on with it.

At 8:30 they moved him into the surgical suite. They told us it would take a while to get him ready. The nurse said she would update us.

These are the things they hope to accomplish in this ten-hour timeframe: repair of the pelvis, checking the lower spine for damage, and turning him on his belly to repair and stabilize the impacted vertebrae. If time and ability remain, they hope to stabilize the left leg and ankle as well as provide some adjustment to the right leg/ankle apparatus, providing stability to that portion of the body. He also has a broken nose, so they anticipate bringing him back to the ICU with a ventilator, which will hopefully come out on Thursday.

This will be a day of waiting for everyone: Todd, Erica, family and friends. We know Todd is in the wonderful hands of God's angels who are performing their surgical skills to allow for healing and pain reduction. Thanks be to God for all your support, prayers, and presence. Thank you also for the wonderful notes of encouragement and support. You all are a blessing to us and we thank you all for being a blessing to us. Though the recovery will be arduous and long, we are grateful to God that Todd is still among us and that we have the opportunity to discern what God has in store as a result of this tragic accident. God will provide.

ERICA: 1:30 PM

Hello all,
Our little restaurant buzzer just rang for the update. The doctors say everything is going well—that is all we ask. Only eight to ten short hours to go! Go Todd!

ERICA: 4:30 PM

We are rejoicing as Dr. Ly just finished the front side of the pelvis. No surprises, it went very well. They flipped him over, and the neuro just started. We will give updates. Your prayers are being heard!

ERICA: 8:42 PM

We just received an update: Todd is stable and doing great, but it is going to be several more hours. They are working his back and are concerned with some nerve damage in his foot. The nerve in his spine may have become detached: if so, he won't get that back. If they can salvage that nerve, he has a 50/50 chance to get it back.

If the nerve is detached, it means that he can't press down on his foot, like when you press on the gas pedal. I am sorry, I am a little twitty right now, but things are going as well as can be expected. The doctors haven't had any surprises and Todd is fighting on!

Thank you for all of your prayers today. The Lord worked wonders with those surgeons' hands.

ERICA: 9:53 PM

Praise the Lord, the doctors just finished! They did as well as they could do. They weren't able to repair the nerve but, like the doctor said, if that is the worst of it he is very lucky. He will have to undergo the surgeries for the legs later.

Thank you for all of your prayers today. The Lord worked wonders with those surgeons' hands. Thank you Lord, thank you Lord, thank you Lord! Now everyone get some sleep.

Love to you all!

GUESTBOOK:

Dear Erica, family and friends,

It is early, Erica. You know how difficult it is to get a good night sleep with the two loves of our lives in such a broken state. As you and I both know, God is working many miracles here at Regions. I truly believe God has sent his angels to be there at their sides.

My prayers are going up for Todd as I write this. My heart just breaks for him and his beautiful family. These things should not have happened, but who are we to question the Lord's plan? You know, Erica, the Lord will be with him and all his loved ones through this very difficult and crucial surgery.

I added Todd into Ron's journal last night so our network of family and friends can pray him through his surgery too. I have been blessed with many wonderful people in my life that truly have a strong connection to heaven. Todd will not be walking through this alone. Take strength in that.

May the Lord be with Todd. May He hold you all in the palm of his hand.

With heartfelt care and concern,
Ron's wife, DeLaine (Dee) Rebeck

———

Thinking and praying for you all day today.

The kids have a body book that we look at, and we were looking at all the bones yesterday. They know that Mary, Timmy, and Madeline's daddy is in the hospital and so I showed them all the bones he had broken. As I read them off I cringed. I cannot imagine how much pain you must be in. I sat in amazement that you are still here—it was not your time, thank God!

Erica, thank you so much for keeping us updated. I hope you have been able to rest. You have a lot on your plate as well, ask if you need anything!

All our love and prayers for both of you,
The Boyles

———

Todd and family,

It has been a long time since St. John's and FLHS, but we never forget good people. We are relieved to hear about your progress Todd, and wish you and your family the best as you recover.

Dan and Melissa King

LOOKING BACK...

Even with the pain medicine I couldn't sleep. The ventilator had been removed a few days ago: that was a little victory. I hated that ventilator! I was more concerned with that contraption than I was with the surgery.

I thought about the surgery. Just do it, Todd. Just finish it. I knew this was one step among many that would be required to recover.

No surprises, please.

DAY 8

ERICA: 10:05 AM

Good morning all! The doctors decided to do surgery on Todd's left leg this afternoon, so they are going to keep him intubated. His nurse said that when they bring him out of sedation he follows commands, but they will keep him out until whenever. It may be a long day today again, but I will keep you all updated.

ERICA: 11:33 AM

They changed their minds: no surgery until tomorrow. Thank God! He went through enough yesterday. They will keep him under today for more healing time.

ERICA: 11:31 PM

Hello everyone. It is late Thursday night. I love updating the journal before bed because I feel like I am saying goodnight to 3,782 of my closest friends.

I knew I was lucky to marry Todd, but have only recently discovered the magnitude of that luck. As our pastor talked to me today, I realized that most of us have people that come in and out of our lives for whatever reason. But everywhere Todd has gone he's never let anyone go, he just keeps them in his back pocket!

My am I happy he does that! Every one of our family is reaping the rewards of his ways: the prayers, the food, the money, the certificates, the house cleaning, the list goes on. It is too much for words. Thank you!

Todd was kept sedated all day. They tried to extubate twice, but his body wasn't ready yet. He finished first in a marathon yesterday, so I guess we'll give him a break. There was some thought of operating on his left leg tomorrow, but the doctors are going to hold out until next week. They will give the wounds on his leg more time to heal, so they have less chance of infection.

The nurses have all said that when they move or jostle any patient with severe wounds like Todd's, those patients will scream out in pain. But not Todd: he quietly takes it. Don, Eunice, and I were watching the nurse adjust his leg today. She lifted it a little and we watched Todd come up from sedation, open his eyes, crinkle his forehead in pain and lay back down. It was heartbreaking: the nurse even had to wipe a tear away.

They tried to extubate twice, but his body wasn't ready yet. He finished first in a marathon yesterday, so I guess we'll give him a break.

I am praying for a peaceful night for Todd. My dream is to get to the hospital with him sitting up, waiting to say he loves me! I miss hearing those words. If you know Todd and I, we say it each and every time we get off the phone or leave each other.

Thank you again for all your love and support. I will report in as soon as I get to the hospital!

Love to you all,
Erica

GUESTBOOK:

Praise the Lord! What a champion and what a miracle.

God bless you, Erica, for your strength and faith: Todd is so blessed to have you by his side through this tough time.

The prayers are coming strong to you all from Forest Lake every minute of every day.

Love you,

Lynn and Hammer (Greg Kienholz)

Know that we will be diligently praying for all of you at this time. It is a very stressful time for you with questions that sometimes have no answers.

Our hearts are hurting for you, but we know that with the Lord directing all that is happening, you are in the best hands possible. Looking back over the past four years since my accident, God has orchestrated so many things to happen in His timing, not mine. Don't let yourselves be discouraged.

Isaiah 40:31 (NIV) "But those who hope in the Lord will renew their strength. They will soar on wings like eagles; they will run and not grow weary, they will walk and not be faint."

What does it mean to hope in the Lord? The word hope implies both trust and patience. Trust involves confidence in God's power to deliver and faith that He will keep His promises. Hoping in the Lord also implies the patience to wait for God's promises, since God works according to His own timing.

God knows what is best for us and when it is best. He will never let you down! We will continue to keep you all in our prayers. God bless each one of you.

Diane and Ron Hammes

LOOKING BACK...

I spent this day in a haze of narcotics. I don't remember any of it.

FRIDAY, JUNE 13, 2008

ERICA: 12:58 PM

Alleluia, alleluia! I was anxious to get in this morning, but it took me a little bit to leave the house. I got here a few minutes before 11:00. Visiting hours close from 11:00 to noon. I quickly shot in the door, flew down the hall, and walked in to Todd's room.

He was sitting up, eyes bright and ventilator out. What a wonderful sight! He has the BiPAP mask on, but at least he is able to talk a little. The doctor said he can have some water and juice to drink, so he was anxious to drink that. For all of you that know Todd, you know he is incredibly driven. I leaned in to hear what he wanted to say. He said, "Five days ago."

Of course I didn't let him finish and I said, "No, it is eight days ago today."

He crinkled his eyebrows and said, "Five days ago, I set a goal to have some juice."

I had to raise the glass to him and say, "Congratulations baby!"

I have been here for days watching him, wanting so badly to know what is going on. He's just been sitting quietly as he does, setting his goals. Wow is all I can say. He is doing great today: those prayers are being heard and answered.

For all of you who are willing and able, I would like you to grab a nice pint of Guinness tonight and raise your glass for Todd. He is a miracle!

ERICA: 8:44 PM

I just got home from an unbelievable day at the hospital. Todd is out of ICU, can you believe it? I tell you he never ceases to amaze me.

I know all of you are anxious to see him and talk to him, but I think we have to give it at least through the weekend. He is still groggy, trying to get his bearings. However, as you all know, he is going to need a major cheering section for quite a while. All of your diligent prayers and positive energy are working miracles.

To think where we were last week and where we are now . . . it's amazing.

GUESTBOOK:

Deuce,

I was in Costa Rica last week and got back to the states last night. I found out about your accident from my sister as I was changing flights in Houston to Boston and was running to catch the plane. As I was stuck in a metal tube for three hours, it gave me time to reflect on all the great times we had together at SJU, Asset Management, and with the Minneapolis Lumberjacks as well as time to pray for you and your family. It's evident from all the messages in your guestbook that you've made a big impact in many people's lives, and we are all here to support you and your family. I know you've got a big journey ahead of you, but I also know you can do it!

I remember before the Jack's Championship game vs. the Sting, our coach told us that the game would be like a roller coaster, with highs and lows. The team that won would be the one that could level out those peaks and valleys and stay focused. Well, he was right and we won.

More importantly, I took his advice and applied it to my life. Now Fultz, I give it back to you on this journey. Stay focused, fight with that Johnnie spirit, and win this battle!

Thinking about you in Boston,

#67, Doug Lawrence

———

Erica,

Just read your update. It must almost have taken your breath away to walk into Todd's room to see him sitting up. That is amazing and truly a miracle. You both are remarkable! Let's continue to pray for, as small as it might be, progress with each new day.

Bill and Judy Mansun

———

Erica,

Todd is so blessed to have you as his wife! As I read your updates today I can just picture your energy and upbeat spirit and excitement. I am so happy he is doing incredibly well, and you need to take some credit too. Your love and encouragement have helped him so much. Be sure to take care of yourself as you are going through a lot too. We will continue to pray for your entire family and the continued healing.

You go girl! Keep up the positive vibes!

Janet Parent

LOOKING BACK...

I woke up face to face with the ventilator and immediately asked my nurse when I could be rid of it. She said the doctor would be in to check on me soon—we could discuss it then.

When the doctor came in I knew by the expression on his face that the nurse had warned him. He said he would get it out shortly, and he did.

What's so terrible about a ventilator? Imagine a tube going down your throat and into your stomach. It's the size of a garden hose. I was so glad to be done with it.

I was acutely aware of my condition and the goals of each day. I wasn't able to think much past each day though, as each day was enormous.

DAY 10

SATURDAY, JUNE 14, 2008

ERICA: 1:03 PM

The dance with this healing process is crazy, but I guess that is what you do. Todd is doing OK. As long as they continue to control his pain he is less anxious. The doctors are watching his breathing closely. He is getting a CT right now on his chest.

He may have to come back to the ICU, but we will cross that bridge when we come to it. He watches my face very closely for my reaction to things, so if I am not there in his room I don't want him to be nervous.

Thank you everyone! I can hardly believe the crew at our house today doing yard work! Also, thank you Pastor Kris for the presents for the kids, they loved them.

ERICA: 10:17 PM

I spent the day with Todd. It was nice to be able to sit in his room. It kind of feels like the old show M.A.S.H. up on the trauma unit though. Todd shares a room with two other people—it's not as "luxurious" as the ICU, but Todd is making friends fast.

His breathing got better through the day, so they are just keeping a close eye on it. The biggest issue is that he has been lying flat for so long that he has fluid in the bottom of his lungs. Also he is in so much pain that when it starts to get more intense, he breathes faster.

He did get better throughout the day though. I think he calms down a little when I am sitting there because he isn't quite sure of all that is going on yet. He is staying so positive. I just love him so much. I told him of all the people that have visited his site and he was just amazed and very proud. Thank you again. I just have to say it every time because it is just so wonderful to know that we have such a fantastic support system around us.

Happy Father's Day to all you wonderful men out there. We appreciate all you do!

GUESTBOOK:

Hi Todd and Erica,

I was sorry to hear the news about Todd's accident, but what a miracle. God is sure on your side: apparently you have more things to do here. I was checking up on you today and am really shocked to hear that you are doing so well! Keep up the good work!

Know that I am thinking of you both and your family.

Your favorite framer at Nature's Image,

Barb Knudson

———

Todd and family,

I have been following your updates and thinking about your family every day. I spent this morning at the Farmer's Market in downtown Saint Paul with my four-year-old daughter. On the way home I couldn't help thinking about what you guys are going through just a few blocks away. I really wish the best for you and realize how important it is to *cherish the moments we have with those that mean so much to us. Todd has always been the kind of guy that would take time for a "stop and chat" if he ran into you somewhere around town.*

Keep fighting and great Father's Day!

Vic Murphy

LOOKING BACK...

I didn't know until they moved me from the ICU how much I'd miss the silence there. The rest of the hospital seemed so fast-paced in comparison. Overall I was happy to get out though, as I knew it was the next major step in recovery.

Erica told me that the next day was Father's Day and that she wanted to bring the kids by. It was very hard to be away from my kids. I have been lucky enough to have jobs that have kept me home and given me a lot of time with my family. This time in the hospital would amount to the longest I'd ever been away from my kids.

DAY 11

ERICA: 10:37 PM

I hope all you dads had a wonderful Father's Day. What a beautiful weekend! We celebrated Madeline's third birthday today. It was very nice.

I brought the kids in to say hi to Todd today. They did pretty well: Mary had a few tears, and Madeline had a wonderful smile.

I went back to see Todd tonight and he was having a hard time. The doctor came and saw him and said he probably has some infection around the incisions, so they're going to start him on antibiotics.

> A wise man once said, "It is the surmounting of difficulties that makes heroes." Todd is mine.

Todd is very anxious being in the M.A.S.H. unit. Can't blame him, as they put a drunk guy who was stabbed at the bar in his room last night. The doctor said he could have something to help him sleep, so I am praying hard that it helps him. They switched his mattress to an air mattress, and he said it was much more comfortable.

The one thing that I know for sure is that he smiles at me with his half-lip smile (still swollen from surgery), winks at me, and tells me he loves me. I can live with all of this stuff as long as he does that!

A wise man once said, "It is the surmounting of difficulties that makes heroes." Todd is mine. Tell yours that you love them too!

GUESTBOOK:

Happy Father's Day Todd!
Erica, reading your blog every day has become a source of inspiration for me and so many. I hope you can hear the community around you silently cheer as they read your entries full of faith and hope.
God bless!
Gretchen Perkins

———

Happy Father's Day Todd,
You were in all of our thoughts and prayers today. You are a great dad and I wanted to share a story with you. A couple days ago Ciera and I were hanging out with your awesome kids. Little Madeline was climbing—no, scaling—the climbing rock at Stone Bridge playground. I asked her, "Who taught you to climb a mountain so fast?"
Timmy looked at me and said, "I did."
She quickly turned and said, "Uh uh, my daddy did." Clearly, you've taught your children through your example and continue to teach them by climbing your current mountain. We are all here for you and love you very much.
Erica, don't forget to take care of yourself. (In fact, put down that Diet Dr. Pepper and grab a V8!) You are amazing and are an inspiration to so many of us as we look at our own lives. We're all here for you.
Lydia and JT (Jason Terwey)

LOOKING BACK...

Eleven days since the accident, and we talked about it for the first time. I knew I'd been in an accident, and I knew how it happened. I cringed the first few times I thought about it. I tried to focus on recovery.

It's strange to feel simultaneously lucky and unlucky. I marveled at this oddity of having both of those emotions colliding within myself. What were the odds that I would live? Why did I survive? What was the margin of survival?

I convinced Erica to leave my cell phone with me today. She didn't want to, but I needed it. It was something of mine that I could have in my little screened-in room. My cell phone connected me to my friends and family. I remember scrolling through the names of everyone I knew.

That night I called a few friends. I'm sure they were surprised when my number appeared on their caller ID. I didn't talk long, I just wanted to let them know that I was fighting hard.

It was a night I will always remember. I had never heard so much emotion and gratitude in their voices before. I fell asleep that night with a smile on my face.

DAY 12

ERICA: 9:18 PM

Have I told you yet how amazing he is! I see such progress every day. Todd's attitude is nothing less than incredible. Don, Eunice, and I sat and listened to him recount the accident today. He remembers details that one would never think he could. As he talked his delivery was so calming. He firmly believes that this experience has a purpose, one far greater than most people could comprehend at this time.

He said that when he looked in his sister's eyes and saw fear of losing another brother, looked in his mother's eyes and saw of losing another son, and saw his wife's eyes filled with fear of losing her husband, he knew he had to start the fight of his life! We have experienced that game-winning attitude ever since. I come out of that hospital every day feeling like I just went to an inspirational seminar!

> He firmly believes that this experience has a purpose, one far greater than most people could comprehend at this time.

Dr. Ly, his lead ortho surgeon, was in today. He said, "I love working with patients like you, Todd. You are driven and understand what needs to be done."

Dr. Ly is hoping to do surgery on Friday, possibly on both legs. The swelling needs to go down a little more in the left. As for any infection, they are watching closely, but his blood counts haven't changed and he doesn't have a fever, which are great signs. I am excited to see what tomorrow brings. I will forewarn some of you, though: he made me leave his cell phone!

The prayers are working, keep them coming.

GUESTBOOK:

Todd,

We think about you every day and send out our strongest positive vibes and prayers to you and your family for your super-fast recovery. You're the quality kind of person we don't want to leave the earth too soon. So glad you are going to stick around for a while.

Love and hugs,

Chris (Obst) and Bill Coleman

———

Todd,

You and your family have touched my life since I was a sixth grade classmate of Tim's. Your horrible accident is also a story of inspiration and strength, things you've never been short on. Keep focused on your recovery and your wonderful family. You have so many more hearts left to touch.

You are in my prayers,

Carrie Plantz Krautkramer

LOOKING BACK...

Eleven days since the accident, and we talked about it for the first time. I knew I'd been in an accident, and I knew how it happened. I cringed the first few times I thought about it. I tried to focus on recovery.

It's strange to feel simultaneously lucky and unlucky. I marveled at this oddity of having both of those emotions colliding within myself. What were the odds that I would live? Why did I survive? What was the margin of survival?

I convinced Erica to leave my cell phone with me today. She didn't want to, but I needed it. It was something of mine that I could have in my little screened-in room. My cell phone connected me to my friends and family. I remember scrolling through the names of everyone I knew.

That night I called a few friends. I'm sure they were surprised when my number appeared on their caller ID. I didn't talk long, I just wanted to let them know that I was fighting hard.

It was a night I will always remember. I had never heard so much emotion and gratitude in their voices before. I fell asleep that night with a smile on my face.

DAY 13

TUESDAY, JUNE 17, 2008

ERICA: 8:32 PM

I thought that I would put a more uplifting picture on here! If you don't know the relationship between Jeff Boyle and Todd Fultz, they are two Johnnies recounting the crazy shenanigans that they used to get into when they were at school. I think they giggled from the time Jeff got there until the time he left!

The doctor came in today and again remarked on how Todd is such an incredible patient to work with. Go Todd go!

He is going to have surgery on his legs this Friday. It should be a good portion of the day, but it will be awesome if he can get both of them done in one shot. The doctor said that, if all goes well, he may be able to start rehab next week.

Todd is up for the challenge, you better believe that! Thank you again for everyone's extreme generosity and support. I am so, so thankful to each and every one of you.

GUESTBOOK:

Wow! Shouldn't you look like crap when you are lying in a hospital bed for a few weeks? You look great and it is nice to see your smile. Ross and I are happy that things are going well for you. Keep it up! Erica, hang in there. You are also in our thoughts and prayers.

Jean Schrankler

Hey, this is Amy from your favorite restaurant, Not Justa Café. Just wanting to send out my thoughts and prayers to your family, and Todd you better get your butt better to make more appearances in that cute bear costume at our fine establishment. (To anyone who reads this, keep the costume secret from the kids.) We miss you.

Erica, take care of yourself and those beautiful kids of yours.

Love,

Amy Seibert

LOOKING BACK...

It hurt to laugh. My stomach was in pain as my abdominal muscles flexed.

My dear friend, Jeff Boyle, visited me. It didn't take long to get the old stories and one-liners going. I was ready for a good laugh after the past few weeks, and it really helped me feel better.

My surgery appointments were being rearranged then, but I desperately wanted to get it over with. The sooner I finished with my surgeries, the sooner I could begin the recovery process.

It was on that day that I became aware of the complexity of my surgery. There was not much left of my right ankle, and I could see in Dr. Ly's eyes that he was concerned about how much he would be able to do.

A heavy thought, thinking that my ability to walk again was resting in this man's hands.

DAY 14

ERICA: 11:04 PM

Another really good day! Todd is just busy doing everything he can to prepare for surgery on Friday. He has also figured out that if he gets to know everyone's name and a little something about them, he gets some more prompt attention when he needs something. Just like Todd, right?

I was busy reading the guestbook to him today. I was just taken aback, because whenever I read an entry, he would go through and tell me exactly how he knew you and a little something about you all as well. He was so touched by everyone's well wishes. Lots of tears of gratitude today: he is so appreciative.

We ask that you say a few extra prayers on Friday so everything goes as well as it can. Then he can get busy healing! I will keep everyone updated on the progress.

Hope you all had a wonderful day.

Love,

Erica

I would also ask that you put a family I know in your prayers that tragically lost their son on Saturday. They are having his funeral tomorrow. Please pray that they can find some peace in all of their sorrow.

GUESTBOOK:

Petitions for healing and patience continue. God's continued blessings with each of you.

The sunshine has been glorious these past three days. "This is the day that the Lord has made, rejoice . . ."

Peace,

Gwen Hansen

———

Todd and Erica,

We are sorry to hear about your accident. We think about you every day. So glad things are going well.

Great updates Erica! It's the first thing we do every day, even before the morning paper. Todd, when you're up for it, Scott and I will take you to lunch at the Village Inn. (It will always be the Village to us.) Wait . . . I will take you to lunch because Scott won't bring enough money.

Hope your surgery goes well Friday.

Bruce and Andrea Grant

———

Dear Todd and Erica,

Yes, our extra prayers will be with you for Friday's surgery. Thanks, Erica, for your journal entries. Todd has a great partner!

As noted earlier, Duane is a cousin of Don, knowing Don (and then Eunice) for a long while. Duane and his first wife welcomed Todd when he was adopted in Sioux Falls years ago.

The first week of June was a hard one for us. Besides Todd's accident, my daughter Linnea's fiancé was injured in a bicycle accident on June

2. We feared the worst, but he is now recovering with broken neck vertebrae and broken ribs. His life was saved by his helmet and there seems to be no brain or spine damage. Though he's in a neck brace (and probably using a walker) they will be married on schedule in North Branch this Saturday.

Steve, too, has a can do spirit.

Duane and Eva Addison

LOOKING BACK...

I will always remember this day. Erica printed some of the CaringBridge guestbook entries and read them aloud. The magnitude of the responses shocked me. I was amazed at the outpouring of entries from around the world and the power of the words that were written. The emotion of the moment poured out.

When the car hit me, I didn't cry. When I had a ten-hour surgery, I didn't cry. Now, as I heard the words of encouragement and love from my friends and family, I bawled my eyes out.

I was proud of my life that day.

DAY 15

ERICA: 8:23 PM

I am sitting here next a very conked out Fultzy! I am not kidding you, he had time slots filled today with groups of visitors. I got here this morning and he ran down the itinerary for the day—the nurses cracked up laughing. But seriously, thank you for everyone who stopped by today. He will be out of commission until early next week.

I will give updates throughout the day though. He is doing well, but I think the adrenaline is starting to wear off and he is much more tired now than he was at the beginning of the week. I am spending the night tonight so I can be here bright and early tomorrow morning for surgery.

Thank you all for those prayers! Worldwide, it's incredible!

GUESTBOOK:

Dear Erica,

So great to see the pictures of Todd! My mom said she saw you and gave you a big hug from me too.

I think about you all the time. If there is anything I can do, you know how to reach me. I want you to know that you and Todd are truly inspiring. Through sharing your story, you have opened people's eyes, and made them realize what is truly important in life. I will be praying for Todd tomorrow. As you know, and I have said before, the doctors there are amazing. He is in great hands!

Love to you,
Sara Sofie and family

Erica and Todd,

It was great to get the update and see the new pictures. Todd, you are an amazingly strong, motivated person. It was great to see you in the photos. Good luck tomorrow with the big surgery ahead of you. Of course my thoughts and prayers are with you tomorrow.

P.S. I spent the day with the kids. They are the coolest kids I've ever met. It was a blast. Love you all.

Mary Furseth, or ahhmi (ahm, as Madeline has been calling me)

LOOKING BACK...

It's tough the night before surgery. So many thoughts ran through my brain, and sleep seemed worlds away.

I woke up the night before my last surgery and stared at the wall for an hour, thinking. This was to be my last surgery, so at least I had that going for me.

DAY 16

TODD: 9:38 AM

Good morning everybody, it's Todd! I am getting ready to go into surgery.

I am optimistic that the doctors will be successful today and that I will be on the road to recovery soon. I am overwhelmed and humbled by the love and support that I have received over the past two weeks. Your stories, emails, words of encouragement, and the memories of the days of youth keep me going.

> I am optimistic that the doctors will be successful today and that I will be on the road to recovery soon.

Please remember Dr. Ly today in your prayers. And also please remember Ron, the man who hit me, in your prayers as he recovers as well.

As many of you have mentioned in your stories about my life lectures, life is about friends, family, your passions, faith, and your experiences within. I am so grateful for not only the experiences that we have had together, but for many more to come. Thank you again for everything, and God bless you!

ARAM: 2:01 PM

Hi all!

Erica asked me to update everybody on Todd's surgery. As of 2:00 pm the surgeons are still working on his right leg, but he is doing very well. Needless to say, nobody is surprised that he is handling this round like a champ.

It sounds like they are hoping to get to the left leg soon and that he could be done with surgery around 5:00, but that is up in the air. Erica promises she'll make sure there is an update on here when he is done. Keep Todd in your prayers, they've been a tremendous help so far!

All the best,
Aram

ARAM: 3:33 PM

Hello again.

Erica just called and asked me to post another quick update. Todd's surgeons just switched over to his left leg and are beginning work on it now. Todd has stayed very stable through the entire surgery and it sounds like everything is going perfectly.

Erica anticipates at least another couple of hours, so keep those prayers and good thoughts coming!

ERICA: 9:02 PM

Amen, amen, amen, amen, amen, alleluia! That is the song that is playing in my head right now. Dr. Ly has just finished and he said Todd did great! He said, "He has some strong bones!"

They put four plates in his right leg and a number of screws in the left. Dr. Ly said that, with Todd's determination and the support of his family and friends, he will do great.

He is now on the road to rehab. We will know better on Monday or Tuesday when and where that will be. Thank you so much for the worldwide prayers today, they worked miracles! I am going to tuck him in when he gets back to his room and call it a day.

GUESTBOOK:

To Todd: At the risk of being that name you know but can't quite place the face, I have to send you my well wishes. I don't think there's anything I can say that friends and family haven't already said. The love is merely a reflection of what people see in you! I believe God has used you to reconnect our hearts with great hope and determination. Thank you for taking on the task. Lives have been forever changed!

To Erica: This feels so strange. We have never met. (My loss completely!) Grace pours from your heart in every journal entry. Because of that, you give amazing perspective and put much-needed contentment in the lives that are just bumpin' along. Thank you! There are hundreds (and thousands) of women you've never met out here supporting your every step of the way!

To Pastor Fultz and family: We just finished Holy Trinity's Vacation Bible School this afternoon. Had you and your family on my mind all week. Your fingerprints are everywhere there. Bless you for your commitment to Christ then and now!

With much love,

Tasha Topka-Kallal

Todd,

I was catching up with Walter's columns today and saw the story about the accident and was stunned. Thank God you are okay.

It is so odd as I was in New England just the other day, thinking about you and the Minnesota/Boston football deal we did together in Ireland and what a great time we had. I was thinking I needed to call you to get together and have a pint.

Robin and I are praying for you and your upcoming surgery. It's wonderful to see the pictures of you smiling: of course I would expect nothing less because you're always smiling.

When you are up to it, please send us a note. I will call you as well. Something like this is a good reminder on how precious life is, and how one can never take friendships for granted. It's been too long and I look forward to reconnecting. Stay strong and in good spirits.

Your friends,

Sam and Robin Richter

LOOKING BACK...

I wrote on the CaringBridge site for the firs   a June 20. It was emotional and I struggled to get the word   . It overwhelmed me to broadcast to so many people who had prayed and supported my family and me for these past couple weeks.

Before the surgery I spoke with Erica about my condition. I didn't have the feeling that anything was being kept from me, but I wanted to make sure. I asked my wife a tough question: "Have you and the doctors told me everything about my injuries and my condition?"

It was so quiet when I asked. For a moment I feared there might be something I wasn't privy to. Erica assured me that I knew everything she did.

I remember thinking I could overcome this challenge. I thought of my kids at that moment and that I was going to fight to be the dad they used to have.

As they wheeled me out of my room that day to prep me for surgery, I was motivated and excited.

DAY 17

ERICA: 3:31 PM

Todd is having a lot of pain today. Yesterday's surgery was successful, but took a lot out of him. He ended up going back to the ICU last night, but was able to be transferred into trauma this morning. They saved his spot for him. It was so busy last night that it took a long time for him to get a room. I'm hoping the pain subsides a little or that they are able to control it better.

Ron Rebeck had a heart attack last night, so if you could please send some extra prayers his way, that would be terrific.

Also, send some prayers to those that are running Grandma's Marathon this weekend. May God provide them with the energy they need to cross that finish line. I will be thinking of you all. What a beautiful weekend.

We are hoping to know more midweek about what the next step is for Todd. He will be off to rehab, but we will have to make some decisions on where he will go. I just pray that Todd can get some rest this weekend, and that he will be much better on Monday.

GUESTBOOK:

Hey, Elmer Fudd here. Glad to hear your surgery went well. We've been thinking a lot about you down here. We've talked about putting a deer stand on a man lift to get you up high enough to post, and then having a heater in there as well. Can't miss hunting!

Stay strong—like that was ever an issue.
Our best,
Jay, Sheila, Nathan, and Elizabeth Fultz

———

Hello Todd and family,
It's Mary Amundson Bahneman (John and Kelly's mom, former next door neighbor in Forest Lake).
We are all so very sorry to hear about your accident. I can only think of that very strong, handsome young boy that we watched grow up to become such a wonderful man! You can and will do this with grace and strength as you have done with the rest of your life.
Remember the cute story you told me when you had just moved into Forest Lake from New Prague? You told me with a very large teasing smile while dribbling a basketball all over the driveway that you were an adopted kid and that your biological father was a man of color, and that is where your athletic talent originated. Your mom, with her usual loving ways, just said with a large laugh, "Todd!"
I also remember your silly pranks as a kid. Remember how you crept up next to my car in the garage and grabbed me around the neck? It was late at night and I was going to pick you and John up at the movie theater downtown. I always check around the car before I get in now: great lesson you taught me!
You will be in our prayers. God bless you and go Todd!
Sincerely, Mary

LOOKING BACK...

The days after surgery are quite eventful, but mercifully unmemorable. They kept me drugged up.

DAY 19

MONDAY, JUNE 23, 2008

ERICA: 4:26 PM

Hope that your weekend was wonderful. Todd was pretty down and out all weekend. The surgery took a lot out of him, but it's all over. No more surgeries that we are aware of. He is really tired and uncomfortable, and understandably so.

We talked to the social worker today about the next moves. Basically as soon as he is able to start some of the rehab stuff we will know better when he will be able to get out of here.

Of course Todd has a plan for everything. He really wants to go home instead of transitional care. The social worker said it is possible, but there is a laundry list of things that would need to happen to make that possible. Of course Todd replied that we will do everything we can do to get that ready.

So we will see: I need to get a hold of a construction worker and some other people to get ready. He really misses not being at home with the kids and me. He said that being home will make him better faster. I want the best for him, so whatever everyone agrees on will happen. Keep those prayers coming: his spirits weren't as high today and I want him steady.

As the famous Mr. Gagliardi once said to Todd, "There are going to be highs and there are going to be lows. The key is to stay centered, right in the middle." Good advice, and that is what we are working on.

Todd also said that he appreciates everyone's well wishes, but he isn't quite ready to see anyone right now. I gather that if he does come home in the near future, we will need a lot of help. So, for all of you waiting in the wings, we'll be calling soon!

GUESTBOOK:

Todd and Erica,

Sorry to have dropped in on a tough day, but I felt like I needed to visit Todd in person and let him know how much everyone is pulling for him. Todd, it was great to see you and to talk to you today. You have an awful lot of fight in you and you understand the big picture. Keep listening to your docs, your wife, your kids, and your friends and know that the Johnnie family has you all in our prayers.

Pete Amann

———

Todd,

Glad to hear the surgeries went well. The one thing you need to keep reminding yourself of is not to take it too fast. Recovery needs to be only as fast as your body can tolerate.

I know you will be in a hurry, but let the body determine the speed versus your mind. We all know you have the will. You've come a lot farther than anyone (other than you) could imagine in such a short time. Your faith and strength and family have made all that possible. You know everyone is pulling for you. Get well soon, your wife and children need you at home.

Tom Paul

LOOKING BACK...

My legs ached after the surgery. It was much more painful than the back surgery. I would cringe when people walked by as even the breeze inflicted pain.

I remember meeting with the social worker to ask about skipping transitional care and going right home. I got a call a few days earlier from Ron Hammes, a very dear friend whose wife, Diane, was also in a terrible car accident. Ron advised me to avoid a rehab center as it might not fit my personality.

So I asked the social worker what would be required of me to go home. She said, "First you would need to prove to me that you can transfer to a wheelchair from your bed."

I said, "No problem." (In retrospect, I may have been a little overconfident.)

Next she told me I would need a handicapped-accessible house. Again, I said, "No problem." Finally, she said I would have to be able to take my own medications at home. "No worries," I assured her.

I should have asked for more clarity on that last condition. I wanted to be home so badly, I figured I would be willing to do anything.

Great, I thought. I've got one day to plan for a miracle.

The social worker said she would be back the next day to do the transfer. Great, I thought. I've got one day to plan for a miracle.

DAY 20

ERICA: 6:32 PM

Good afternoon everyone. Hope you all are doing well.

I can't believe that it will be three weeks on Thursday. Time doesn't stop, does it? Like Todd says, one day closer to getting better. I met with my good friend Kipp Ronning today. He owns a construction company and he is going to help me with some of the things that need to get done for Todd to be able to come home.

Each day is a gift as we embrace our "new normal" together.

Todd still isn't medically ready: they were pushing for Thursday of this week, but there is no way. He worked with the physical therapists today, transferring himself from his bed to a chair. After a couple of laps around the unit, however, he was pooped. He has been pretty wiped out the rest of the day from all that action.

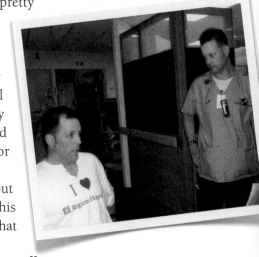

They all said how impressed they were. They didn't think he could do all that on the first try. They obviously don't know Todd very well: he is always up for a challenge.

He was very happy about it. He tells me daily what his positives were. You know what he says: "If you aren't positive, you aren't in a good spot." He is so great at making good out of every situation.

We still need to hold out on visitors, though. He is just so exhausted that it is hard for him to hold a conversation.

Each day is a gift as we embrace our "new normal" together.

GUESTBOOK:

Hi Todd,

It looks like you are taking giant steps to a full recovery. You don't know me, but Erica and I shared some anxious hours in the ICU waiting room. You are so fortunate to have such a loving and strong wife. Although she was worrying about you she took time to comfort me when things got rough.

I am returning to St. Paul tomorrow to visit my daughter and can't wait to see Erica and Dee and the others in our support group. I'm also anxious to hear firsthand about your progress. The last time I was with Erica you had just gone through fourteen-plus hours of surgery. Looks like you came through that with flying colors.

Keep up the good work. Know that you are in my prayers.

Marie Doucette

LOOKING BACK...

"Okay, I hear you are going to prove to me you can transfer to a wheelchair to get out of transitional?"

I felt like my physical therapist was calling my bluff, which certainly motivated me to prove her wrong. She showed me what I needed to do: to sit up and use my arms to move me to the edge of the bed. From there I would lift my body and slide myself to the wheelchair. My legs didn't work at all and it hurt if I bumped them. Thus, I depended entirely on my arms: my triceps, to be exact.

I was not strong in the arms to begin with and I had been lying in a bed for the past three weeks, which does nothing for muscle tone. I tried to get myself to the edge of the bed, and it was very tough. By the time I managed to move myself a few inches it felt like I'd run a marathon.

By the time I managed to move myself a few inches it felt like I'd run a marathon.

My arms trembled as I started to lift myself to the wheelchair. My mind raced as I balanced my legs in this awkward position. I'm sure my face showed how challenged I was, but I refused to be denied.

I knew I had one chance to do this. I gave it all I had, made one big move, and managed to land in the wheelchair. "See?" I said. "I told you I could do it. So this means I can go home, right?"

She replied, "Yes you can, but you need to transfer back to your bed."

Wait a minute—nobody told me this was a round trip!

My arms felt like they were going to fall off. Fortunately my physical therapist said, "Why don't you wheel around the wing of the hospital for a moment?"

Great, I thought. This would buy me some time to recover. And it did, but more importantly, all the nurses cheered as I came out of the room. It really motivated me, and I did get myself back into bed, even if it was less than elegant with a lot of flopping and rolling involved.

In the end, I passed the test. I was totally spent, but I was proud!

DAY 21

ERICA: 10:26 AM

Can you tell Todd is sick of being in the hospital? His physical therapists are so impressed with his ability to transfer to a wheelchair. He is going great guns to prove to them that he is ready for the next step.

We are working hard at home getting ready for him. The hospital bed and miscellaneous other things should be delivered by the end of the week. I will keep you in touch with the expected ETA for the Todd Fultz homecoming!

Go Todd go!

GUESTBOOK:

Hi Todd,

Wow, what amazing progress you've made! The new photo of you is awesome. We've been watching your website daily and praying for your continued healing. By the notes in your guestbook, it sounds like your persistence and strength are pretty much the norm!

I see Riitters left you a note today also. Tom and Katie are close friends of ours (fellow CSB/SJU alum). What a small world!

Todd, Kenny, and I wish you all God's blessings in your healing process and continued strength and patience for your family as you recover *at home. It appears that you've got a fabulous support system and your wife sounds like a wonderful gal! Looking at the photos of your car on the website, you are a living miracle! God must have big plans for you.*

Sending our best wishes and prayers from New Prague,
Sara Zweber

———

Erica,
Your enthusiasm and perseverance is equal to the strength of Todd's determination. What planet are you two from?
Judy Gulden

LOOKING BACK...

We made plans to go home. I figured I can lie in a hospital bed at home just as well as at a transitional care center. I was so excited to be around my family and to look out the windows and see our backyard.

DAY 23

ERICA: 7:44 AM

He's ready! He has passed all of his tests with flying colors, so Todd is coming home tomorrow!

He wouldn't go to the nursing home, so the nursing home is coming to us, and Ronning Construction and Langer Construction are making it all possible. Thank you for all your continued prayers. Todd's spirit, strength, and determination are so strong because of all of you.

I am going to make a schedule for those who would like to volunteer to hang out with Todd. Let me know any of you who would be interested in taking like a four-hour block.

Thank you, thank you, thank you. He will heal much better at home!

GUESTBOOK:

Fultz,

Glad to hear you are going home. As you continue your rehab, remember the immortal words of Smitty: "If I had another point guard, I'd play him!"

We'll have to get together soon for a little game of check-check.

Patrick Carey

LOOKING BACK...

I was finally cleared to go home. What a great feeling! My time at the hospital with those three surgeries had been very challenging. I knew there was a long way to go, but it was comforting to know I would see my family every day.

I remember being a little sad to leave my favorite nurse, Amy. She was such a key person for me these past few weeks. I would miss her great sense of humor and her genuine concern for me.

I said goodbye to the other great nurses and staff that day. It was emotional to say thank you as they had all cared for me and I had been so dependent on them.

DAY 24

SATURDAY, JUNE 28, 2008

ERICA: 3:32 PM

The day has finally arrived—Todd has come home! We have him in the downstairs living room. I think he will be much better here, it will just take a few minutes to get used to the kids climbing all around him. So far we haven't had any fights with who gets to ride the wheelchair, but I imagine it's coming. I am in the process of setting up a schedule, so look for that update.

I am sorry, I do need some more help though. I am calling on all handymen and women. We have a flooring issue that we need to resolve in short order: anyone who could assist with that in the very near future could you please e-mail me? Thank you so much!

Other than that, thank you for those prayers that helped get him home. Now we are on to the next phase!

GUESTBOOK:

Todd,

What a joyful feeling to be sprung from that hospital! I met your wife at the hospital about a week ago. Her love for you shone through. I told her your father was our pastor for many years. She said you have a son named Timothy. Our son, Aaron, will always remember when your brother Tim took the blame for a broken ceiling light fixture at church. Our prayers are for your continued healing.

God's Blessings,

Rich and Ellen Hoiland

LOOKING BACK...

Almost four weeks ago, I arrived at Regions in an ambulance in excruciating pain, not knowing if I would ever walk again. Today I left, proud of my time here and scared of what lies ahead.

I lifted my hands in the air when they wheeled me through the front door. My body hurt. I was weak but glad to be going home as they wheeled me into a transport van.

The prospect of being in a vehicle again made me nauseous and jittery. My father rode with me, a comforting presence. As we turned toward Stillwater, I started to feel at home. It was great to see the familiar buildings.

As we turned down my street and my home came into view, I started to cry. Erica and the kids greeted me in the yard, rushing to me as they wheeled me out of the van.

Inside they had my room set up: everything was great. I could see out the front window from my bed, and I could also see into the backyard.

I was home.

DAY 27

SUNDAY, JULY 1, 2008

ERICA: 11:28 PM

Hello everyone! Wow, what a whirlwind it has been since Saturday. This is the first chance that I have had to update. Todd is doing well. I know he is very happy to be home. He still has quite a way to go though.

The count is on for his rehab, hopefully around September 20. He is still very uncomfortable and has a lot of pain. I'm just trying to help him relax a little.

Don and Eunice have been over helping out a lot. We are so grateful for their help. If anyone wants to take a 2:00 - 4:00 shift any time, just let me know. Email me, and I will tell you what it would entail.

I hope you are all doing wonderfully. Have a great 4th of July!

GUESTBOOK:

Okay, guys.

Now the hard part comes. You have a lot of missed worship services to make up for. Zanny and I will be over soon to lead you through the songs. We will sing all the verses! Consider it part of your rehab.

There will also be an Elvis impersonator, and a couple of Ty Pennington moments. We have missed you guys. The place just hasn't been the same without you.

Phil Kadidlo

LOOKING BACK...

How strange it was to sleep in my house without my wife. It was comforting to know my family was right upstairs, but I felt lonely nonetheless: so close and so far away.

Those first few days were tough. I worried about how to manage my pain and give myself shots. I had to give myself two shots a day, one in the morning and one at night. It took fifteen minutes to do it, and everyone had to leave the room. When they returned, I would be in a complete sweat.

Even with that, I was glad to be home.

DAY 29

SUNDAY, JULY 3, 2008

ERICA: 9:57 AM

08-08-08, Save The Date!
WHAT: Todd Fultz Benefit-Silent Auction-Appetizers-Cash Bar-DJ
WHEN: 7:00–10:00 pm, August 8, 2008
WHERE: Water Street Inn, 101 Water Street S, Stillwater
WHY: To help defer medical costs and get Todd back on his feet!

We are organizing a benefit for Todd and his family to help defer medical costs and get Todd back on his feet. Appetizers, a cash bar, and a DJ will be on hand. A silent auction will be held to include sports memorabilia (obviously!) as well as other items of interest.

Tickets are $20 per person in advance or at the door.

To ensure that we get an accurate headcount for the Water Street Inn, we prefer if you would RSVP with a check and the number of people in your group to either Todd Zapzalka or Jeff Imsdahl. Checks should be written out to Todd and Erica Fultz. Cash is also accepted and tickets can be bought at the door the day of the event.

The Water Street Inn is in downtown Stillwater at the corner of Water and Chestnut Street. If you have questions, please call either Jeff or Todd at the numbers provided!

ERICA: 11:48 PM

Happy 4th of July!

As you can see by the last journal entry, a few of Todd's friends are having a benefit in August for our family. I thank Todd every day for being such an awesome guy to have so many people who love him. We hope all of you can come so we can share many hugs with you all. The prayers, the well wishes, and the support have really gotten us through this

Todd went in today and got the splints off his legs. His legs are so skinny, it is crazy. His ortho doc fit him with boots that he will wear for a week, and then he won't have anything on his legs.

The doctor is also weaning him off all of his narcotics. He is able to take 1,000 mg of Tylenol now. He is doing OK, but his right leg is causing him a lot of pain.

Dr. Ly looked at his films this morning and was pleased with his healing. Dr. Ly is a perfectionist, and that's a real blessing to us. He is positive but also realistic when he talks to us. We feel we are getting the absolute truth from him—sometimes we haven't felt that with other doctors.

One of Todd's friends, Mike Sonntag, really came through for us, replacing all our flooring. He and his father own Abbey Carpet & Floor in White Bear Lake. He brought three guys out and got it all done. We are so grateful!

Also, thank you for all of you handypeople out there that have offered to help us out. We will keep your names at the ready—it is amazing how many little things keep coming up.

I am going to get a calendar together for all of you who would like to take a shift with Todd. It will be so nice for Todd to have some new help. I will get this together this weekend.

I just want you all to know how much we love you all! Have a wonderful weekend, and we will talk to you soon!

GUESTBOOK:

To our dearest old neighbors:
You are in our deepest thoughts and prayers during this time of healing. May the warm breezes of summer and beautiful light heal your hearts and home.

With loving prayers,
Paul and Karina Peterson

Hi Todd and Erika,

Just your favorite place checking in on you. All the girls on the Trauma Unit say hello and hope all is well at home. Don't be a stranger: stop back as soon as you get better.

6-East Trauma rocks!

Angie Sparrowgrove

LOOKING BACK...

Together with Doctor Ly we looked at my legs. Doctor Ly always gave me such encouragement, but even so
. . .

Oh, those legs. They looked like sticks. Ugly ones. I can't believe the legs that helped me run fast in high school and college are gone. I remind myself that I'm lucky just to have survived the wreck.

> I remind myself that I'm lucky just to have survived the wreck.

I decided then and there that I would run again one day. It wouldn't be a pretty sight, but I was determined to do it.

DAY 35

TODD: 5:40 PM

Hello everyone, this is Todd.

I am so grateful to be here. I feel very lucky.

I am so thankful for all of you and for the many great messages and stories that you have sent. They keep me going.

> I continue to get a little better each day and focus on only the positives. It is the little victories in each day that will get me through the next few months.

I continue to get a little better each day and focus on only the positives. It is the little victories in each day that will get me through the next few months.

I want to say thanks to my parents who have basically lived with us since I came home. They have been a tremendous help.

Also to my wonderful wife, who has been amazing. I am so grateful for all she has done. Love ya E!

I hope you are all doing well. It looks like a great summer. I can't wait to see all of you and give you a big hug! Keep the messages and stories coming!

GUESTBOOK:

Todd,

I've added a couple of messages out here, and I'm not even sure if you remember who I am.

I was a classmate of Tami's and Chuck's at FLHS. I remember you as Tami's incredibly nice big brother who always seemed very happy. I can tell your "happiness factor" still remains. That's awesome!

I wanted to share something with you and Erica about an experience my husband and I had together recently. During the past three years, my husband has had two major surgeries to correct a congenital heart defect. There were days that we would be at the hospital and at home thinking, "I wonder if the worrying, the recovery, and the chaos will ever end?"

Yes, we would try our best to stay positive as best as we could externally, but inside there were just those days . . . I'm sure you know what I'm talking about.

What I want to tell you is this: the strong moments you've had throughout all of this are fantastic, so keep it up! At the same time, remember that it's OK to have a weak moment or two also. You're human!

Just keep marking the days off on your calendar as you move towards getting back to your "new normal," as I believe Erica called it at some point in these journal entries.

You will heal! You will heal! You will heal! Continue to hang in there.

Heidi (Kertzscher) Harvey

LOOKING BACK...

Independence Day was great, but a tough night followed. It was humbling.

The next day I was feeling better. I left the window open to feel the warmth of summer, something that had been in short supply in the hospital.

My nurse and therapists came almost every day. I had a regular nurse, a physical therapist, and an occupational therapist. Though the work they did often caused me a great deal of pain, I was thankful for it and for them. Weaning off the narcotics made the slightest movement in my legs painful.

I knew I was traveling down a long road. I found something positive each day, focusing on that thing to get by.

DAY 37

FRIDAY, JULY 11, 2008

TODD: 10:19 PM

Howdy!

Todd again. I'm taking over for Erica as she is on a short break. Erica and Mary and Papa David are in Texas for cousin Pete's wedding. Mary is the flower girl. Timmy and Maddie are at Grandpa John and Grandma Judy's for an overnight, so it is quiet here. My parents are staying with me and we had a good day.

Each day gets a little better. I am doing my rehab twice a day. I'm doing motion-related exercises for my legs and ankles, trying to maintain a little strength, so once I start trying to walk I will have something to start with.

I have to be off my feet (no pressure on them) until September 20, and then I can start the process of walking again. I can't wait to start trying to walk again—it will be like the first couple weeks of football and basketball when you get the leg burn. I know it will be a while and I will only go as far as they allow me.

I have always believed that something good inevitably comes from something bad. There have been a few things already, but the most impressive is the love I feel from everyone.

> I have always believed that something good inevitably comes from something bad. There have been a few things already, but the most impressive is the love I feel from everyone.

It has been such a rewarding experience to find out how many people are pulling for you and how kind and generous they are. I am amazed at the level of love and concern. It is humbling at a level I cannot explain.

An example of this (and there are many) is how all of my close buddies responded in the exact same manner. These are my football, basketball, fishing, and hunting buddies: tough guys. Each one of them on their first visit and each visit since has uttered three words that I had never heard from them before: I love you.

Can you imagine these guys saying that? Wow.

Life files by so fast and takes us in different directions, but something like this brings us back together. What a gift to see and hear from all my friends and family, to feel the love at a level that had not been reached before. I wish everyone could experience this—without the crash and pain and rehab, of course.

I got an e-mail today from Bishop Mdegela of the Iringa Diocese of Tanzania to let me know that all seventy parishes would be praying for me this Sunday at their worship services.

Then I got a call from my good friend Tony Seeley in Lurgan, Northern Ireland to check in. I received calls from a number of local friends and family, and a few letters and e-mails. A few of my workers stopped by to give their best. Then I went to my Caring-Bridge site and read the recent letters.

You give me such strength!

It is so awesome to know that I have a huge team around me. We are going to make a great story of this and I thank you for being a part of this ride!

I've got a great story for you tomorrow night, see you then.

GUESTBOOK:

Todd,

I saw Mike Grant today and heard you are home and beginning the recovery process. I enjoyed reading your update: your attitude will take you a long way as you begin this journey to recover. My brother had some similar injuries as you two years ago and he is doing great.

My prayers have been with you and your family since I heard of the accident. You are obviously blessed with a tremendous support group of family and friends. I hope to talk with you soon.

Tal Gravelle

———

Hi Todd,

I talked to Craig and JD at our QSP meeting and they filled me in on your predicament. I want to add my get well soon.

Someday I'll talk to you about a successful carnival company that I'm running. I'm a carny!

Good luck with your rehab. You have a great looking family!

Dave Haines

LOOKING BACK...

I had been home a couple of weeks. On this specific day, I was alone except for my parents. I felt strengthened just knowing I was at my own house. The quiet set in, but it was the kind of silence that empowered me instead of depleting my energy. This was my home, I realized—and to be here, even in the quietness, I felt stronger and more capable to handle the challenges ahead.

This period was a turning point for me. I felt an independence that I didn't feel when the doctors or Erica or the kids were around. I was looking out for myself, and that freedom felt great.

DAY 38

TODD: 10:10 PM

Good evening. Todd here, filling in for Erica. Your favorite reporter will be back tomorrow.

The wedding went well and Mary did great as the flower girl.

I just wanted to share a little story with you about how our priorities can overpower our fears. Ever since I can remember I have been afraid of needles and shots. When I heard I'd be getting one, I'd go lightheaded. I would ask the nurse where it was going, how long it would take, and if she was any good at it. I made it a habit to ask nurses how many shots they had given to patients in their career: if the number was less than 200, I'd ask for a veteran to take over with the needle.

Many times I needed to lie down after the shot before they would let me leave.

After the accident I got a lot of shots. You could always spot me getting the shot, as I was the one with the blanket over my head. And yes, the nurses had a good laugh at my series of questions.

> You could always spot me getting the shot, as I was the one with the blanket over my head.

When they said I would be moving to transitional care, I wanted to know if I could go home instead. They said no because our house was not handicapped accessible and I had not transferred to a wheelchair yet. I asked if I could go home if I made my house accessible and successfully transfer? They said yes and I was so excited.

Erica and I made some calls and got the home ready. I made my wheelchair transfer the first try, although I had to give it everything I had. The nurse came in and said, "You are all set to go home in a few days. I just wanted to go over your meds, which will include giving yourself two shots each day."

What! Where did that come from? Instantly I was hit with cold sweats—I might have to rethink this deal. Then I saw a picture of my kids that I keep on my bed, and in a moment the priority of being with my wife and kids blew the fear of shots right out of my mind.

I asked the nurse to show me how to do it. After the brief training she said, "Here, why don't you try?" I looked at her and said I would.

I gave myself a shot that day and have done so each day since then.

GUESTBOOK:

Todd,

Your needle story is a riot. I laugh because I am exactly the same way and I am married to a nurse! I remember the first shot they gave my son Sam (now eight) two weeks after he was born. Holly sent me to the doctor with him and the nurses had to sit me down after I watched them poke my son.

Glad to hear you have overcome your fear, maybe you can pass along some pointers. When I see needles, I still run the other way!

Mike Sonntag

LOOKING BACK...

A strong sense of priorities has the ability to erase lifelong fears. How incredible is that? Under the right circumstances, your mind doesn't think, it doesn't process—it just *reacts* to what's right, to what you want. And I *wanted* to be with my kids. I *wanted* to be in my house. I *wanted* to be with my wife.

When I was presented with the option of returning home instead of going to a transitional care center, I didn't think twice. I jumped at it.

There was a catch, however, and it was sizable. As it turns out, the ability to transfer myself from bed to wheelchair and back again—Mount Everest-sized feat that it was—was actually the least of my worries.

Before I could go home again, I'd have to come face to face with, and master, my worst fear.

We all have these situations. We have a longtime fear but at some point we make a change. We move forward, no matter what the stakes.

DAY 41

TUESDAY, JULY 15, 2008

ERICA: 10:37 PM

Hello all! Victories, victories: we are celebrating today! With the help of his aide, Todd was able to take a shower. I told him that his month and a half beat my record and not to tease me again. He laughed.

I think he may also have hit his head because he laughs at my jokes now.

He finished the antibiotics he started last week for a staph infection. It seems to have cleared up quite well. All in all I think that we have adjusted to our new arrangement at the house. Eunice works hard with Todd twice a day—you can really see the progress he is making in his flexibility and range of motion.

Also, our guy received more press with his accident. Bert Blyleven wished him well during the Twins game on Sunday!

I ask that you all say a prayer tonight for my friend Zanny and her family as her sister passed away last night. Pray for comfort for them as they go through this tragedy. We love you, Zanny.

Thank you to those people that have donated such special things for the silent auction. Unbelievable, there will be lots of great things there.

Love to you all. Your prayers are so awesome!

GUESTBOOK:

Dear Todd and Erica,

It was great to be in your home today and to spend time with the two of you! Todd, you are making such positive progress. (Though never as fast as you would like, I'm sure.) It's hard to imagine all that you have been through these past few weeks. The way you are making the best of it is inspirational to the rest of us. It was great to see your parents again as well.

It's hard to believe twenty years have gone by since you were leading our team as point guard for the Rangers! I was blessed to be able to coach you and so many impressive guys at FLHS. The infectious smile and neverending enthusiasm of #20 that carried our team are the same qualities that will take you through this challenge as well. Talking through some of the good old days today was a lot of fun.

I look forward to seeing your improvement each time we meet now. You are in the thoughts and prayers of our entire family. Penny sends her love. See you soon.

Brian Hegseth

LOOKING BACK...

The task that lay ahead of me seemed so simple: taking a shower. I knew I could do it, but the transition from my wheelchair into the shower was an epic battle, and the pain in my legs as the bandages were removed was intense.

The nurse that helped me was patient, calm, and encouraging. I was so nervous. I hadn't showered in a long time and I felt incredible anticipation as well as independence.

The process was humbling. Getting into the shower took five minutes and I needed the guidance of the nurse to complete the transfer. Once inside though, I felt relief and familiarity wash over me. I smelled the comforting fragrance of our soaps and shampoos, and I started to relax. The nurse left me alone then.

The warm water felt so cleansing. My skin was incredibly sensitive from being wrapped and untouched for many weeks. I began to cry, one of the few times I let myself do so over the course of my recovery.

It was a triumph—it was a leap.

DAY 46

TODD: 4:30 PM

Each day gets a little better. Each day little victories!

I focus only on the positives in each day as my legendary college football coach, John Gagliardi, taught us. At St. John's, when we watched game films John would only let us watch the great plays or, as he called them, "the classics." We didn't watch mistakes.

That approach creates a confidence and positive attitude that you *will* succeed because you have seen yourself do it. John is the greatest coach in the history of college football but, more importantly, he has given the thousands of kids who have played for him even better coaching in life. And just as it has helped me I hope you are, or start, using it as well. Focus on your "classics" each day and don't worry about the small stuff.

I am getting in my wheelchair four times a day for about forty-five minutes each time. I do rehab in bed three times a day. It is mostly range of motion and strength training. I am sleeping through the night. There are still challenges each day but not as many as before.

It is just great to be here!

Today is the end of my first month of staying off my feet. Fifteen more days and I'll be at the halfway point! Then a few days later I will get to see many of you at the benefit—I have a lot to look forward to.

It is a beautiful day today. I hope you are enjoying it! Thanks again for everything.

GUESTBOOK:

Todd,

Thanks for your inspirational update. It was a beautiful day today, indeed. (Wish I hadn't spent it inside working on taxes!)

I talked to Erica at Zanny's sister's funeral yesterday. We marveled again at your can-do-it-ness! I think I need to hang around you and let that kind of positivity rub off.

You are a lucky man to have played under Coach John. My dad was the football coach in Hudson for twenty-some years and had that same positive approach. Unfortunately he retired right about the time I would have had him for a coach, and the guy who replaced him was the complete opposite. That was my last year of playing football. (I shouldn't have been playing high school football anyway, given that I play piano and beat my hands up playing offensive line. Duh!)

I look forward to more updates.

Phil Kadidlo

LOOKING BACK...

I had been home almost a month now and I could feel momentum building. My victories were happening more easily and more frequently.

My gratitude to John, my old football coach, was so great as I wrote this entry. Focusing on the positive things in life is so crucial. Negativity is easier to see and to feel, and it can consume you.

I'm grateful that I took the more difficult road, adopting a totally optimistic perspective.

DAY 53

MONDAY, JULY 28, 2008

TODD: 10:37 PM

Little Victory #342: No surprises at the doctor's office!
I went to Regions today for my appointment with Dr. Ly.
He is incredible. He went over all of my X-rays with me, so I have
a good handle on my injuries. I will definitely get the special pass
to go through any metal detector now . . .

No major surprises, just plowing forward with rehab and
healing. The journey continues. In five weeks I will go back and he
will give me more of a specific date as to when I can begin walking.

We are so grateful for the nurses and doctors at Regions who
have really gone above and beyond for me.

Thank you for all the wonderful things that you have done for
me and my family.

It is so rewarding to be around family. It is amazing how much
you grow together when you have the time to be together. It is
time you never regret. I hope you are finding the time in this
busy life to be around those you love. I've been blessed with
another three months off work to spend at home. I will look back
at these recovery days with fond memories: a little bit of pain
but a lot of love.

GUESTBOOK:

Hi Todd,
Sounds like things are coming along for you. I am glad to hear it.
I am looking forward to seeing you and your family on 08/08/08.
These hot summer days sure remind me of Forest Lake and being kids
with no real concerns other than swimming and a game of capture the
flag! I wish things were that simple again. Soon they will be.
Kelly Amundson Beaudry

LOOKING BACK...

The doctor's words were something I was both afraid and desperate to hear. I was full of hope—hope that my body was responding in the way it was supposed to.

Doctor Ly is such a gracious man. He says I am his "favorite train wreck" every time we see one another. He would tell me I was an ideal patient because I was so positive and determined to handle whatever curveball my condition threw at me. This was the key to a victorious recovery.

It was significant to see him because he had literally built my ankle, so he knew what its capacity was. He understood my situation better than anyone, and to get compliments and encouragement from the architect behind my healing—this felt enormous.

DAY 56

THURSDAY, JULY 31, 2008

TODD: 9:30 PM

Hi! Todd here. How are you doing? Is your summer going well? I hope you are having a blast!

Having a good day today. Yesterday was a little tough as I was not feeling well, but we got through it. Took a walk tonight with the family. It was nice to get outside as I have been stuck inside with this weather.

Today I did two interviews: one for the *St. Paul Pioneer Press*, and one for the *Stillwater Courier*. The *Stillwater Gazette* is also doing an interview on Monday. I believe all three stories will be in Tuesday's paper.

It is very exciting to hear about all the people coming to the benefit. It will be one big reunion! I have heard that they will have a live auction with a special auctioneer: George Thole. Look out!

I plan on being there and look forward to seeing you.

Yesterday Erica and my dad went to do a final check of my car before the insurance company takes it away. I am grateful to the person who designed the car as they did a great job. I think each day about how lucky I am. It is great to be here!

I'm looking forward to Tuesday, as it will be the halfway point to start my first steps.

I read some good stories this past week: keep them coming. I love to hear them as they bring me back to those good times.

GUESTBOOK:

I'm thanking God for His goodness in preserving your life. You have a special purpose for being here.

Reading your journal on CaringBridge is such an encouragement. May God continue to bring healing and courage to you as you face each challenge.

May He help your family as they show love and support to you in countless ways. May He also bless your many friends!

Livija Ford

LOOKING BACK...

It's been raining. A lot.

I stared out the window at the downpour, feeling troubled about what condition I might be in for my upcoming benefit party. So many important people in my life had given me their support, and this event was going to be a tribute to them. I didn't want to just make a ten-minute appearance—I wanted to celebrate with everyone that mattered most to me. I wanted to show them that their love and prayers were helping.

The buzz and hype around the benefit party was tremendous. How often do we see this broad a scope of our friends and family all at once? Marriage brings together a large number of people, but aside from that, it's very rare.

I was so lucky to have this experience. My whole life would be spread out before me in a sea of familiar faces. I had to be fully present for it.

DAY 60

MONDAY, AUGUST 4, 2008

TODD: 9:47 PM

Hi everyone, it's Todd.

Just wanted to take a moment to share again how precious our life is.

A few days ago our family lost a very dear friend to breast cancer. Her name was Jill (Hines) Roiger. She was one of my sister's best friends growing up and our families spent a lot of time together. Jill had a dynamite smile and always a kind word.

On June 9 Jill wrote me on this site to wish me well. I remember, she said, "Wow, was God looking out for you!"

I am thankful for that message. I have gone back to it many times over these past few days.

Our family's thoughts are with Jill and her family.

God bless you.

ERICA: 10:13 PM

Hello everyone,

Friday is quickly approaching, and we are so excited. It will be so fun to see all of your faces and give you big hugs in person as opposed to e-mail. I just wanted to let you know that children are more than welcome to come. They can shake shake shake on the dance floor! See you all on Friday.

GUESTBOOK:

Fultzie,

I think we should race on the 8th. I've been working out and I think I might be able to give you a run for your money!

Seriously, I'm glad to hear you have started the recovery process. I wish we could see you on the 8th but I am tied up with a Twins game that evening. Can we buy tickets even if we don't attend?

Be well, our family's thoughts are with you every day.

Anthony LaPanta

LOOKING BACK...

I watched others going through pain and sickness at the same time I was. It's a strange feeling, this sense of injustice. Why was I getting better while a friend's condition worsened?

There's no logic to it. No matter how hard I tried to wrap my mind around it, I couldn't understand why people like my friend Jill became more and more sick as I got better and better. I guess I got dealt the best card in the worst pile.

> I guess I got dealt the best card in the worst pile.

I struggled to accept that others in our group of friends were fighting just like me to overcome illnesses and injuries. It was very hard to watch while some friends slipped away and others surmounted the obstacle. When you're struggling, you have a special connection to other people who are struggling.

The whole thing was a weight on my chest. I didn't sleep well that night.

DAY 61

TODD: 11:04 AM

Hello,

Todd again. Today is a great day! Today is the halfway point of my recovery to begin walking again. The finish line is in sight, I can see it in the distance.

In only fifteen days I will be down to one month!

The weather looks great this week so I plan to get outside each day.

I am grateful for this opportunity and can't wait to see you Friday.

I hope you are all doing well.

All the best,

Todd

GUESTBOOK:

Hello everyone!

Just wanted to let you know that we will not be able to attend on the 8th. Our family will be on a quick getaway before Mal heads to college and the boys start football practice. I wish we could see you guys in person: it sounds like so much fun!!

I was working out a week or so ago in our local fitness center and I looked up at the TV and there were the both of you on the Decorating Cents episode! I couldn't believe it! You guys did a nice job.

I've been sharing your story with many in the Tracy area, and I know you are an inspiration for us all. Hopefully we can connect with your family on one of the trips we will be making to St. Paul for Mallory.

Have a fantastic time on Friday, we will be thinking of you all!

Love,

Sandy Fultz

LOOKING BACK...

The weather hoisted me up onto its shoulders. This brilliant energy lasted all week.

DAY 62

TODD: 1:28 AM

Hey again,

Todd here. It's after midnight and having trouble sleeping 'cause the Twins just lost to a guy named Putz! How do you lose to a Putz? Oh well.

Seriously though, I had another great day recovery wise. A week ago I thought I would be at the benefit for about an hour, but now I think I can do two hours.

I have been able to stay up longer in my wheelchair and the pain these past few days has gone down. I have had seven good days out of the past eight.

This coming home thing has really done wonders.

It is so rewarding to be around family. It is amazing how much you grow together when you have the time to be together. It is time you never regret. I hope you are finding the time in this busy life to be around those you love. I've been blessed with another three months off work to spend at home. I will look back at these recovery days with fond memories: a little bit of pain but a lot of love.

> It is so rewarding to be around family. It is amazing how much you grow together when you have the time to be together.

ERICA: 9:35 PM

Just wanted to update you that Todd will be on the radio to-morrow morning on KSTP 1500 AM on Thursday morning at 8:35.

Also, he had a big day in the papers with three articles in the *St. Paul Pioneer Press*, *Courier*, and the *Stillwater Gazette*. All so nice, we really appreciate all the kind words. Does this guy get some press or what? I can't imagine his days as a football star!

GUESTBOOK:

Todd,

I hope you are feeling better. It sounds like it is good to be home around family. Our thoughts and prayers are with you and your family. I was made aware of your accident by Dean Simon: we were friends and teammates in high school and play golf together quite a bit now.

It's funny, I ran across a photo of you and I at the science fair in grade school—after looking at some of your photos online it doesn't ap-pear that you've changed that much. Obviously I haven't seen you in quite some time.

Well, I hope your recovery goes well. Again, my thoughts and prayers are with you and your family.

Best,

Keith Krouse

———

Hi Todd!

While paging through the Pioneer Press *yesterday, the photo of your sweet family caught my eye and I learned of your heroic efforts to help in Hugo and extraordinary survival following your accident on the way.*

Then this morning, I heard your pastoral voice on 1500 AM!

Both of your interviews reminded me to live with gratitude, love and purpose, much like your unforgettable presentation at our church legacy dinner some time ago. I read through some of your CaringBridge essays this morning as well. With humility, kindness, and wit, you continue to pass on wisdom for us all.

That Erica is a wonder, and can those kids get any cuter? I am planning to attend your benefit on Friday. I hope there is room for me! You have a lot of admirers . . .

Thinking of you,
Jackie Nelson

LOOKING BACK...

The benefit was fast approaching, and I needed to start my "training" in preparation for it. I pushed myself to stay in my wheelchair for longer periods to gain endurance. I was so excited for the event, and I put all my energy into priming myself for the party.

I considered the fact that the next time all of these people gathered together could be for my funeral. While I was above ground, I was anxious to enjoy the moment, celebrate, and see everyone dear to me.

DAY 63

THURSDAY, AUGUST 7, 2008

TODD: 11:56 PM

I think Jack Buck said it best: "And we'll see ya tomorrow night!"

GUESTBOOK:

I heard Mick is taking money at the door tonight. Check his pockets when he leaves.
Looking forward to seeing you and your family.
B. Grant

LOOKING BACK...

It was midnight and I couldn't sleep because I was so excited for the next day. The thrill of showing everyone how far I had come since the accident—how everyone's support had helped me do that—the feeling overwhelmed me.

I needed to tell everyone something: I'm here. I'm alive. I made it. And together we're going to make a good story out of all this.

DAY 65

ERICA: 11:06 PM

Todd and I are sitting here, twenty-four hours after the event and are still awestruck over all the love and support we had at the Water Street Inn last night. We are the luckiest people alive!

We just want to thank everyone who attended, donated, and helped make the evening a success. Our only regret is that we didn't have enough time to talk longer to each of you. But just seeing you there filled our hearts with joy. Todd is able to take more visitors now, so if you are interested in coming over to visit just give us a call and we will find a time.

Also, we will post pictures when we get them back from the photographer. I know you Johnnies will love to see how handsome you all are!

Thank you again. We will always be grateful to all of you!

GUESTBOOK:

Todd, Erica, and family,

What an event last night! It was great to see all the love and support you guys have. We will keep praying for a speedy recovery. If you need anything please let us know.

David and Mary Wolf

———

Good morning, Todd and Erica.

Well, what can we say? Friday night was amazing. You know the old saying that "what goes around, comes around?" Wow.

Todd, you must have done some wonderful things when you think about all the people who were there last Friday. You could just feel the love and support for you and Erica in that room.

I am excited about the items we got in the silent auction. One was a small area rug that is a wintery scene with Frosty the Snowman. We will think of you often when we put it out this winter.

You had to be exhausted on Saturday. Friday was a big, but probably long, day for you. Thanks for letting us share in the event with you.

God bless! Judy and Bill Mansun

LOOKING BACK...

The benefit came at me full force. I had been used to sitting quietly at home, then suddenly I found myself thrown into the presence of so many loved ones. Being in a public space was something I hadn't felt for weeks. I felt stimulated, alive, fully present.

I remember speaking to the larger group, thanking them for coming and trying to express my gratitude. I spoke quietly, but said what I wanted to say. Then I called my dad up to the microphone to give a benediction. As a kid, I loved hearing my dad do this part of the sermon on Sunday. His presence was so calming. I was excited for him to speak to everyone at this benefit, thanking everyone from the heart: "May the Lord bless you and keep you. May the Lord make his face to shine upon you and grant you peace."

I rode the positive energy of my many guests for about two hours, at which point a wave of fatigue swallowed me. It was a kind of exhaustion, however, that I welcomed with open arms.

DAY 68

TUESDAY, AUGUST 12, 2008

TODD: 11:40 PM

Todd here.

Wow, was that awesome! What a night. Thanks to everyone for that amazing benefit. I was overwhelmed by the turnout. I wish I had more time with everyone but it was great to see all those smiles.

I will always remember that night.

I am counting down the days to August 20, which will put me at one month until I can start trying to walk again.

I have been working very hard at rehab to give me the best shot. I have to try and get the most out of what I have.

Today I played basketball with the kids. It was great, as Mary can "hit 'em from downtown" as she says. Timmy is so close to making one on the big basket. He is very determined. I have to beg to get him to pass me the ball. He always says "after this shot, Dad." And little miss Madeline just dribbles all over. She is very talented.

I have to tell you how rewarding my nights are. Each night for bedtime we gather in my room with the kids, Erica, and my parents who come to help each day. We say our prayers and sing some songs and tell stories of growing up. The kids love grandpa's stories of the farm and ask lots of questions about the names of

all the animals. It is so peaceful for that half an hour with no TV or cell phones on. It is time well spent. I hope you are also finding the time with those you love.

Goodnight,
Todd

GUESTBOOK:

Hello Todd! Greetings from New Prague.

We've been watching your progress and are constantly amazed by your positive attitude, determination, and faith. You are truly an inspiration. We will continue to pray for your complete healing and successful therapy sessions. We would have loved to join you for your benefit—sounds like it was a great time! Maybe there'll be another one down the road that we can attend, perhaps to celebrate your recovery as you walk and dance on your own!

May God continue to shower you with little victories. Best wishes to you and your wonderful family.

Kenny, Sara, Luke, Libby, Matthew, and Jacob Zweber

P.S. - Maybe we could send our little Jacob over to keep you company at night. He's teething and doesn't want to sleep either!

LOOKING BACK...

We live in a world filled with TVs, iPods, and cell phones. We're always plugged in. What happens when we turn off these devices and focus on face-to-face conversation? How do our lives benefit?

> For me, my favorite part of the day became the time right before bed. This was time devoted to sharing stories, talking, reminiscing, and praying.

For me, my favorite part of the day became the time right before bed. This was time devoted to sharing stories, talking, reminiscing, and praying. It was time to acknowledge all the good in our lives. These will be conversations that my kids are going to remember when they get older—moments with their parents and grandparents that were genuine and real, without the interference of a phone ringing or the white noise from a television.

Going through this recovery period was never easy, but I wouldn't have had this time to simply talk with my children and learn the value of that had I not been in this situation.

DAY 71

TODD: 12:09 AM

Hello night owls, Todd here.

Can't sleep tonight, but I don't really care because I am already in the bed I need to be in tomorrow.

Thank God for the Olympics. I am looking forward to the coverage of the State Fair coming up as well. Think of all the weight I won't put on this year by not going to the fair and eating all that stick food. Yet another little victory!

> Can't sleep tonight, but I don't really care because I am already in the bed I need to be in tomorrow.

Today I had a hard rehab session that left me worn out. My physical therapist was very excited about my progress. Sometimes just the slightest improvement is exciting.

Seven days to only one month left! Can't wait.

I love you guys! Thanks for everything!

Todd

GUESTBOOK:

Good morning, Todd, Erica, and family,

Petitions for continued joy, progress, and patience. Thank you for the sharing.

I was enjoying a session of the Olympics in which the gymnasts shared their skills after the "medal events" were complete. I thought of you, Todd, when the music and movements were most inspiring. I remembered you breakdancing on a small carpeted area at the entrance to the auditorium in Forest Lake High School. Life is full of wonderful memories, hopes, and joys.

I also enjoyed the words you wrote about sharing communion with your community. God's continued blessings to each of you.

Peace,

Gwen Hansen

LOOKING BACK...

Watching the Olympics gave me a series of inspiring and motivational stories. I tuned into the games as frequently as I could. I felt buoyed up by the great biographies from so many incredible athletes. Their stories gave me encouragement when I considered my own challenge.

Putting my story in perspective with these others helped me move on.

DAY 77

TODD: 12:14 AM

Hi team. We made the one month mark today! It's downhill from here.

I just got the pictures back from the benefit and they are awesome. I got a bunch of good-looking friends and family! What a great time.

I have to get the pictures formatted to put on the website and hope to have them back this weekend. I will put up different pictures every few days.

I shot baskets with the kids tonight in the driveway. We had a great time. Then we went on a walk. It was such a nice night tonight with that breeze.

A quick story from last week: my pastor, Kris, stopped by to say hi as she has done many times since the accident. During our visit my mom asked her if she could bring communion to me during her next visit and she agreed. I thought for a moment. "No, I will come to you," I said. "I will come to the Lord."

> I went up for communion that day with my family as I have done so many times in the past. I have a feeling that I will remember this one forever.

That next Sunday I went to church for the first time since the accident. We were a little late but, as I wheeled down to my seat, Pastor Kris saw me and gave me a big smile. I went up for communion that day with my family as I have done so many times in the past. I have a feeling that I will remember this one forever.

GUESTBOOK:

Todd, Erica, and family,
You are such an inspiration to all. I keep checking back for your up-dates and am always excited when there is something new there. What a great communion story. You are doing great. Just wanted you to know you are in our thoughts/prayers.
Kris (Thomson) Zell and family

LOOKING BACK...

Wheeling myself into church to receive communion with the rest of the congregation, I remember locking eyes with Pastor Kris. I sensed her pride in me, and I recognized then that we can push ourselves harder and farther than most of us give ourselves credit for. It's a choice.

I had considered having the body of Christ brought to me, but instead I summoned the strength to meet the Lord myself.

I'm so glad I did.

DAY 79

TODD: 10:37 PM

Hi everyone!

Todd again. What a day today was. Beautiful!

I am hitting the dog days of rehab. The work has increased and I feel it. I keep my iPod handy to help get me over the hill—thank God for Van Halen! (I bet some of you thought I was going to say Richard Marx.)

Just wanted to share a little conversation I have been having with Madeline lately. She is sweet, and she can only pronounce about half her words so she talks cute too.

Lately when I do something nice for her or she would hear good news about me, she would come up to me and give me a hug. Then she says, "Daddy, you can come to my birfhday party." She has invited me about ten times—I laughed about it with Erica for the past week until I realized what she meant.

We have always asked our kids, "Who are you going to invite to your birthday party?" And, for one of the first times, Madeline realized she had ownership of something. It happens to be one of the most important things in her life, her birthday party. And she is willing to share that with me.

It is a privilege and an honor to have that invitation. It makes me think about what I have that is dearest to me: am I doing a good job of sharing it with those around me? We all have gifts, talents, inspiration, and time. And sometimes it just takes an invitation (or ten) to a three-year-old's birthday party to put it all in perspective.

Thanks Madels, I can't wait for your birthday party next summer!

God bless,

Todd

GUESTBOOK:

Hey Todd,

Just wanted to let you know what an inspiration you have been. I am sure you have some really hard days, but it has been such a blessing to read your journal, hear some of your struggles, but hear your great faith and encouragement also!

There have been times I have been having a hard day and I read your entries and it just puts things into perspective. So, though you say we are helping you, please know you are helping us too. Keep it up and keep looking up. God bless you and your family—we are praying for you!

Sharyl Pinkerman

P.S. My four-year-old just invited me to her birthday party and is making initiations for her fifth birthday in January! It is a big event at that age, isn't it?

LOOKING BACK...

During this recovery I have had many moments of enlightenment, and I have understood things that were never clear before. Simple lessons my kids taught me led to an irrepressible need to share those revelations with others. I realized that this online forum was like a stage—when handed the microphone, I found I had things I needed to say. Things that were so basic: letting good people into your life, then granting them inclusion and trust.

Maybe I knew these things already, but conversations with my three-year-old helped me rediscover these truths.

DAY 80

TODD: 11:24 PM

Hi! Todd here. What a great day today was: we had two picnics on the deck today, brunch and dinner. It was so nice out. I had fun watching the kids play in the yard.

I am very lucky to be recovering at this time of the year. If this would have happened in the winter I would have gone nuts. I probably would have tried to tie skis on to my wheelchair and get outside. Hey, I might have been ready for the winter Olympics—wheelchair downhill!

I shed a little tear tonight as the Olympics came to a close. The games have been a constant companion these past two weeks. It was great to have something good to watch at 3:00 am when I couldn't sleep. The great moments have inspired me and given me many great memories.

One thing that stuck out to me was how long almost all the athletes have trained for this moment. As I thought about it, I realized that we have all trained very hard and long for our moment too, but our moment happens every day. It is being a great parent, spouse, and friend. It is helping those around us and being a good role model. It is our passions and experiences, our faith, and our legacy.

So our "moment" happens all the time and we are constantly training for it. And the best part is we all have our gold medals! Our medals are our family and friends, experiences and passions, and our faith and legacy. We have them, all of us. Some are shinning bright and some need a little dusting off. But we have them and we wear them around our necks every day.

I think of three of my gold medals that run around our house every day or another gold medal that has cared for me these past few months. I am grateful for them. I know you are grateful for yours. You earned them. You practiced and trained for them, and you continue to. And, best of all, they will shine brightly around your neck for the rest of your life.

And, with each day, the opportunity to earn gold again!

GUESTBOOK:

Todd,

For the past several years, this time of year is challenging for my oldest daughter. We call it the "end of summer blues." I love her to pieces, but she was really driving me nuts this weekend!

Then I come in to work today and read your journal entry, and whammo! You totally put things in to perspective for me. You are so right: my husband and my daughters are gold medals and I couldn't wear them more proudly! I guess some days I just have to work a little harder than others to keep the medals shining bright.

Anyway, thanks for reminding me how precious these gifts are and for how blessed I am.

Keep on healing (yourself and us),

Heidi Harvey

————

I was taken by the beauty of the closing of the Olympics too. It's amazing how long and hard the athletes work with their eyes on the goal. I'm sure there are days when they just feel like giving up, not getting up early, not working out, not eating right, but they have to keep persevering in order to win.

Life is that way. We have to keep looking to God and finding our daily strength in Him. We are blessed in so many ways, as you pointed out, and so many times our blessings are those we see and interact with daily.

We still have four young adults at home who are going through so many changes in life—one starts college this week during her senior year in high school. She thinks she's stupid academically, but I tell her no one can excel in every subject.

Another daughter has battled depression as a part of post traumatic stress disorder. She has a daily struggle just to stay alive. Every morning, when I see that she has made it through another night, I am overwhelmed with gratefulness.

Your words are an encouragement to me today to take time to appreciate and savor my blessings. My grandma used to call the grandchildren her "vitamins!"

Livija Ford

LOOKING BACK...

I had a timetable, a goal, and a journey. Pain accompanied me every step of the way. Eventually, I knew there would be one grand victory, but at this point of my recovery I learned that sometimes the victory *is* the journey. The achievement comes as a result of accumulated time and quality exchanges that happen between family and friends along that journey.

DAY 84

THURSDAY, AUGUST 28, 2008

TODD: 12:59 AM

Hey everybody,

Todd here. Just a quick funny story: I told you a few days back about how my youngest daughter, Madeline, is fun to listen to because she doesn't quite pronounce all her words correctly. She is currently working on the letter L.

Her latest and greatest is when she explains to people what is wrong with her daddy.

Madeline says, "My Daddy has two broken eggs."

You should see the looks we get.

TODD: 11:40 PM

Hello again!

It's Todd. I hope this finds you well and enjoying this great weekend!

Things are good here. I continue to be amazed at the wonderful support you have all provided. Each day I receive many e-mails, phone calls, and letters from friends, family, and people I have never met before. I am so blessed by all your kind words. I wish you could all experience this feeling—it is like having a fortress around me. I feel so loved and so protected, for both me and my family. You are all so wonderful.

The past couple of days were tough at times. My right leg just starts screaming out of nowhere and my hips are hurting a bit. I think they want to run!

Otherwise I am plowing forward. I have not had a bad day for about three weeks now. The last two days were only short-term problems and those don't count. Being here each day is a victory.

I am meeting with my doctor on September 4 to see how I am recovering. He has promised me that he will give me the date that I will start "the walking process." We expect it to be around September 20, so we should be down to under three weeks!

I am staying in my chair a little longer these days and moving around a little better. I am training for the September 14 event in Forest Lake. I hope to see you there!

Thanks again for all you have done for me and my family. This has been one of the most powerful times in my life thanks to your support, love, and friendship. I am truly grateful.

God bless you!

Todd

GUESTBOOK:

Hi Todd,

I loved your Madeleine story. I'll share one with you that my Jeff (now fourteen) used to say. I'm sure you know about the book Go, Dog, Go! by Dr. Seuss? We read it at least once a day when the boys were small.

Well, when Jeff was little, he referred to that book as Go, God, Go! I loved that, and it reminds me of you and your family and the faith you are upholding. God is working in you and through you, and your success and patience are truly an example of Go, God, Go!

Blessings to all of you. (Can't wait to see Mary in choir in September . . .)

Gretchen Perkins

LOOKING BACK...

There is so much value in being able to laugh through your troubles and heartache. Just to feel myself smile made me lighter mentally. Children have a gift for bringing out those smiles, even when situations appear bleak. I was so grateful to have some little comedians running around my house.

It's okay to laugh. It's okay to be silly. Often it's absolutely necessary.

It's okay to laugh. It's okay to be silly. Often it's absolutely necessary.

We only get a certain amount of time on this earth, so we may as well have a little fun, no matter what the hardship is that you're dealing with. It's something each of us can afford.

The laughter was essential to me then, as I was battling extreme pains in my right leg at that point in my recovery. I called these pains zingers, and they'd hit out of nowhere. The doctors told me it was normal as my leg went through the healing process, but I worried about how long they would plague me.

A general nervousness set it. I had no idea what condition I'd be in later in life. Not only that, I had to manage the unknown in the here and now—the zingers were an ever-present reminder.

DAY 87

SUNDAY, AUGUST 31, 2008

TODD: 11:40 PM

Hi everyone,

Todd here. What a great weekend this has been. I hope it has been great for you as well.

I am very excited for school to start. Mary will be in first grade this year. Last year she went to full-time kindergarten, so she is ready to get back.

I am also excited to continue a little breakfast tradition in our family. I get up each day with Mary and make her a full breakfast, anything on the menu! We sit and talk as she eats. I love this time as we get a few extra minutes together each day.

I do this because my Mother did this for me. Every school day until graduation, my Mom cooked me breakfast. We would talk as I chowed down and then raced off to school.

I always appreciated this time with her. I loved starting my day that way.

Tuesday, the first day of school, will be special as I am calling in the Breakfast Hall of Famer, Mom, to help out.

I think back to those eighteen years of breakfasts with Mom before school and how cool it will be to start Mary off this year with Grandma and Dad making her breakfast. We are even going to walk her to school after breakfast.

Man, is it great to be here!

God bless,

Todd

LOOKING BACK...

Starting the day with a hearty breakfast and conversation in the kitchen is a tradition I have always been excited to pass on to my kids. When I was a kid, my mom always made me eggs or toast or oatmeal and talked to me about the day before I walked out into the world. I remember those mornings vividly and, during my recovery period, I didn't want my handicap to stop me from getting a good breakfast in my kids' bellies before they left for school.

Making the time for these moments isn't always easy, but words cannot express how important it is. If we don't clear the space for scrambled eggs and bacon in the morning, it won't be there.

Making the time for these moments isn't always easy, but words cannot express how important it is. If we don't clear the space for scrambled eggs and bacon in the morning, it won't be there.

Time is slippery, but it's worth prioritizing for what truly matters in each of our lives.

DAY 91

THURSDAY, SEPTEMBER 4, 2008

TODD: 11:38 PM

Hello team,

Well, I went to Regions this afternoon looking for more little victories. I was anxious as Dr. Ly promised to give me the date that I can begin the walking process. I had been guessing it would be September 20 if all went well in X-ray, though I was prepared that it could be a bit longer.

They took X-rays of both legs and ankles and pelvis, about fifteen in all. He started by showing me the pelvis. It looks pretty crazy since it is held together in three different places by screws and plates. He was very happy with the progress.

Then he showed me the left leg and ankle—he was very happy with that progress as well. Next up was my right leg and what was left of my ankle. It has a lot of metal in it—two rods and a bunch of screws. Once again he was happy with the healing.

So he did some range of motion tests with me and thought about it for a few moments while counting out the days on the calendar. He said "Todd, by September 15 you are ready to start walking again."

It was very exciting. I have spent the past three months primarily in a bed. To be starting the process of walking in just a week and a half is awesome. I will be working out of the Courage Center in Stillwater which will be very close for me.

This will be an exciting time for me as I look forward to the challenge ahead. They are still concerned about the right ankle and the mobility I will have. The hope is that the severed nerve that controls the foot's ability to push off will come back to some degree.

I will exhaust every effort to recover fully, but I am aware that some things may be out of my control. But, as I have seen and heard from my family, they are just glad I'm back at home and with them. For me it's just great to be here.

We scored a few more little victories today. I have a feeling we will start to see them a little more often in the near future. Thanks again for your support and don't forget we are having a walking party before Christmas!

God bless,

Todd

GUESTBOOK:

Wow, what great news for you!

I work at Victory Fitness here in Stillwater, and the childcare that is attached to the gym is called Little Victories. I think of you every time I go into work and see the Little Victories sign outside!

There is a gentleman in a wheelchair who comes to work out each week at the gym. I am always in awe of him and how damn hard he works each day and the fact that he always is smiling. We all are given different circumstances in our lives and I have learned that it is how we choose to deal with them that matters most. Keep up the awesome attitude, and enjoy every "step" you take! You are an inspiration!

Wendy Neurer

LOOKING BACK...

I need goals. I like to have a finish line that I'm approaching, a target to aim for. So meeting with Doctor Ly was pivotal for me on this day. Like any of my great sports coaches, he gave me something to work toward. My next finish line was September 20, and it felt great to nail down an exact date.

My heart sunk though when Doctor Ly showed me my X-rays. I stared at the bits of metal and screws going into the bone in my foot. This was a part of me now. In spite of the tough reality glowing back at me in that X-ray, I took strength from the doctor's confidence that I would be all right and ready to walk by the set date, regardless of the mechanics inside my body.

Sometimes you just have to embrace the truth no matter how difficult.

Sometimes you just have to embrace the truth no matter how difficult. Reality can be harsh, but I would rather meet it head on than hide from it.

DAY 95

MONDAY, SEPTEMBER 8, 2008

TODD: 9:31 AM

Hi everyone!

I was very excited to hear that my high school and college football coach and close friend, Mike Grant, will be speaking at the Forest Lake Benefit at Faith Lutheran Church on Sunday the 14th. It is shaping up to be another great reunion! I hope to see you all there.

I have been working hard on my rehab to be ready to go on Sunday. My rehab is about three times what it was last week. I love it because it means I'm getting close. I can feel my legs getting stronger every few days as my reps increase. It is a powerful feeling to be getting something back that was almost taken away.

> We were never promised life would be fair. We were not guaranteed everything would work out. We were simply given the opportunity to participate in life, and life is full of incredible possibilities.

I wanted to share a little experience I have been having with my son Timmy. Lately when he has been frustrated, he will say "No fair!" Each time I have explained to him to not use that phrase because it is setting him up for disappointment in life. Although he is only four, I want him to understand that things will not always go his way and it usually has nothing to do with fairness. It just has to do with life.

Naturally this made me think about our lives. We were never promised life would be fair. We were not guaranteed everything would work out. We were simply given the opportunity to participate in life, and life is full of incredible possibilities. Each day we wake up we are granted the air we breathe. The rest is up to you. The day is yours.

There are lots of directions to go in and lots of people around us. Surround yourself with the people who find the opportunity in life. They will help you to go places, and in turn you will help them.

I wish we had an unlimited amount of time to get this crazy life figured out. But, since we do not, now would be a great time to take advantage of it. Regardless of what has happened in your life, each day is new and full of possibilities and opportunity. Most of all, it is a wonderful gift.

I encourage everyone to not be a person whose glass half full or half empty—instead be a person whose glass is overflowing!

God bless!

Todd

GUESTBOOK:

Todd,

So glad to see you are doing so well. Our prayers will be sure to double for Sunday! You are amazing and even wiser than you were all those years ago in Forest Lake.

Your Timmy is right—life is not fair—but God never promised that, only that He would be there to help us face all things, good and bad! You are living proof of that.

We love you!

Pam and Dick Landeen

———————

Dear Todd, Erica, and family,

Couldn't help but relate to a statement Bud's 103-year-old aunt Violet made when one of her grandkids said life was not fair. "Fair," she said. "That's what comes in the summer for a week!"

She was an amazing person, as are you, Todd. You've always been able to talk with and show an interest in many people, but your journal has to be an inspiration from God. We do know that things happen for a reason, and sometimes that reason remains hidden or elusive for a long time. Your trials have shown us all how to be so positive and that is just a gift that God gave you to be a light for the rest of us.

Sorry we cannot attend the Faith fundraiser as we had such a good time in Stillwater. Thanks for sending the pictures to us: they're the best ones we've had taken since Forest Lake's 75th celebration.

Love,

Bud and Twink Hennen

LOOKING BACK...

Life can be random and choices can seem few. What counts is that we learn to value what we're given in this world. To me, it's important to be a good role model to my kids; it's important to set the bar high and to move boldly toward what you want to accomplish.

The fact is that we do have choices. We can choose to rise above the challenges and trials at hand.

When I wrote this entry I met with no resistance whatsoever. The words were obvious, the writing effortless. I believed.

DAY 98

TODD: 10:51 PM

Hello everyone,

Hope you are all doing well!

Things are moving along here. I am busy with rehab and very excited for Monday. I have been told that they are going to stand me up with the support bars to see what strength I have in my legs. They tell me that, if all goes well, I could be walking without a walker by Christmas. I'll let you know how things go.

I have been enjoying all the kind letters, e-mails, phone calls, and visits you have made. It really helps me in the recovery. Your support has been one of the most important parts of my recovery. As I approach this final mountain on Monday, I have to stop and say thanks again.

This has been an amazing journey and, while I know there is more to come, I have focused and prepared for this Monday ever since the accident on June 5th. I have thought about trying to walk again every single day of my recovery. It is amazing how much you covet something that has been taken away.

I will have other challenges ahead, but walking will be the big one. As I look up that mountain I can see the top. It may take me a while to get there, but I will. I look forward to the day that I will stand up again and walk on my own power, when I'll look you in the eyes, say thanks, and give you a hug. You have earned it!

I am very grateful for you, for your prayers and your support. And most of all, for helping me to get to this mountain.

I am heading up Monday, see you at the top!

Todd

GUESTBOOK:

Todd and Erica,

I am so moved by the tribute that your Forest Lake friends gave you earlier this evening. I talked to people there that I had not seen for a very long time and to people who I had no clue knew you. I should have known better, since Pastor Don and Eunice reached into the community and were not bound by the walls of their church, and since you and Tami were known and loved by lots of kids and adults. What a tribute to a family!

I am concerned that the whole evening may have been overwhelming and that these efforts at reaching out may be exhausting. However, you are so energizing to so many that it is hard for us not to be perked up by your presence. We really appreciate the fact that you practiced for tonight and that you were with us for such a long time.

Please know that all of us enjoyed being involved and that those of us who are ahead of you in age are relieved and joyful to see the good example you provide to your peers and your children. Chris Berg's message about being a FOCUSed Father fit nicely with your frequent tributes to your family. Mike Grant was lots of fun and symbolizes the significance of teachers/coaches in our lives.

Tomorrow is another day and we pray that you will continue to grow in physical, spiritual, and mental health to meet all the challenges the new day will bring!

Love,

Gena and David Doyscher

LOOKING BACK...

I thought about walking, about getting mobility back. While I was excited, the thought of balancing 180 pounds on my legs seemed impossible. How was this going to work?

Part of my mind was confident that I would be able to swing my legs and walk: the other part told me this was insane.

What could I expect? Would my ankle roll? Would my legs remember the rhythms of locomotion? I remember laying in bed, grappling with so many questions and terrified that I might injure myself again trying to walk.

What could I expect? Would my ankle roll? Would my legs remember the rhythms of locomotion?

DAY 102

MONDAY, SEPTEMBER 15, 2008

TODD: 8:53 PM

Dear friends,

Today was a great day, another little victory. Well, maybe a big one.

I stood up today.

And, with the help of my arms, I made it to the end of the bars and back . . . twice! I don't consider it walking yet (since I needed my arms) but it won't be long. I was very pleased with how today went.

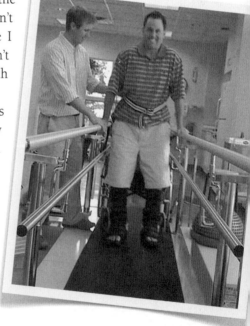

My physical therapist was very excited about my mobility and strength. He said I would be in the pool next week. I am thrilled.

I will be honest—it was scary to stand up. When you have not done it for three months it seems foreign. But I got right up. It was hard to stand straight up though, as my body has not been in that position in a while. It will all just take some time. It was a powerful memory as Erica, Timmy, Madeline, and my mom and dad watched and cheered.

138

When I got to the end of the bars the first time Erica jumped up and said, "I want to hug you standing up!" We hugged. It really felt good. Amazing the things we take for granted each day.

I put a few extra pictures on the photo page to check out.

I want to thank everyone again for the great benefit last night in Forest Lake. It was so good to see everyone and be back at Faith. Thank you to all who worked so hard to put it on. It was a night I will always remember.

Today I took some big steps forward. I felt you all right there with me, just as you have always been.

God bless you!

Todd

GUESTBOOK:

Couldn't wait to see you on your feet this morning! Congrats to you and Erica. You looked very studly standing up so straight! Thanks for taking time to update on the website. Congratulations Todd.

Mark and Sara Krier

———

Thinking of all of as you begin the next chapter in your healing. It sounds like you had a great day.

I have to say, when I read your entries I can't help but think this guy really gets it. Your positive outlook, fighting spirit, strong faith, and ability to tell your story are changing the lives of people who are cheering you on. Thank you.

All our best,

Tim, Cari, Jax, and Ann McGlynn

LOOKING BACK...

Each of us has the capacity to think we've got it worst of all. We can put blinders on and get caught up in our own struggles. When I started going to the Courage Center, I started meeting others who were struggling just as much, if not more, than I was. I felt amazed at their strength and humbled in their midst.

One of my first feelings going into this facility was a sense of guilt and frustration. I knew that I was going to get out of my situation: I was going to walk out of it. Many of my friends at the Courage Center would not have that opportunity.

This realization was something that I had extreme difficulty accepting.

I remember those first steps well. It was like a big, heavy door was creaking open. It felt like bungee cords stretching inside my legs.

I give the others at the Courage Center so much credit because I know what it takes to try to gain a quarter of an inch. My recovery was accelerated in many ways, while theirs were composed of a lot of slow, methodical, minor improvements. They had bigger mountains than what I was climbing at the time.

I remember those first steps well. It was like a big, heavy door was creaking open. It felt like bungee cords stretching inside my legs. I took my first steps (with the help of the bars and my physical therapist). My wife was there to meet me with arms wide open. I was filled with so much hope.

DAY 105

TODD: 11:00 PM

Hi everyone,

Another great day filled with little victories! Today I got in the pool. It was awesome. My body loved it. It was freedom. I could move and stand without much pain. I was able to walk in the water, which felt amazing. It was a powerful day.

Tomorrow I am back on land for physical therapy. I am looking forward to walking down the bars again. I hope to not use my arms as much. It is much more painful walking on land.

I get emotional each time I enter the Courage Center as I realize the potential of the day. The opportunity to take one step without using the bars is right there waiting. I hope to do it soon.

Erica says I get very serious and focused as I start my rehab. It reminds me of game days I guess. I want to win. I want to do my very best. I think of all of you during my rehab and it makes me go! I also think of the walking party. We need to have this walking party before the New Year!

I need to go sleep now as my rehab is scheduled for 9:00 am.

Goodnight and God bless,

Todd

> I get emotional each time I enter the Courage Center as I realize the potential of the day. The opportunity to take one step without using the bars is right there waiting.

GUESTBOOK:

Hey big bro! I have to admit, I've never seen a better picture than the one of you up right now on this site. I check the site everyday and could not be more impressed with your progress.

Love ya bro,

Aram Desteian

LOOKING BACK...

I knew immediately that I would be able to work well with my physical therapist, Kelli. I remember her certainty that I was ready to get in the swimming pool. Her energy was like a security blanket.

Getting into that pool was yet another extremely humbling experience. My body was totally exposed. You could see the scar running down my stomach, which had taken an unusual shape because of the surgeries. My arms were thin, except for these huge triceps from wheeling myself around over the last few weeks. My legs had lost muscle mass too. It was strange to enter into that pool.

Once I was in the water, though—that was a different story. It all happened so fast. What I remember most was how magical the water felt, how warm and soothing. Kelli, a petite woman, picked me up—I was weightless in the water—and brought me to the other end of the pool where I could walk. Actually walk.

The sensation made me cry. I was doing things I hadn't done in four months. I was totally overcome.

DAY 106

FRIDAY, SEPTEMBER 19, 2008

ERICA: 9:27 PM

Hello all! What beautiful weather we are having!

I am filling in for Todd tonight. He is pretty well tuckered out from his rehab, but man is he going great guns. It is so awesome to watch him with his determination. He has often talked to me about his athletic career and the drive you have to have to make a mark for your team. I tease him because I am younger than him and wasn't able to see him play. I really do wish that I had because it seems like I missed out on a truly amazing time in his life. I think that he is channeling those times with his rehab right now.

I am thinking about this because they have a huge link to an event that they are having for Todd tomorrow on the Johnnie football website. I clicked on it and the author talked about Todd during his record breaking days at St. John's. For those of you interested it is really cool to read, www.johnniefootball.com.

> Each day I learn a little something more about Todd. He has been very humble with me about his athletic career, but it seems that I married one of the all-time greats. Well, I guess I knew that . . .

Each day I learn a little something more about Todd. He has been very humble with me about his athletic career, but it seems that I married one of the all-time greats. Well, I guess I knew that . . .

I hope you all enjoy your weekend.

Love to you all,

Erica

GUESTBOOK:

Wow, it's great to see you up again! When we talked on the phone, you mentioned that the doctors said you probably won't be playing basketball in the near future. Well I don't believe them.

Seeing you with the big Fultz smile gives me great optimism that you will do whatever you want to do. You always have. The next few months are going to be harder than any training camp, so keep your spirits high and continue to set your goals even higher. Remember that when the doctors say things, they're talking about the average person. They're probably just learning that, with you, the bar is set a lot higher.

Sam Richter

LOOKING BACK...

The Courage Center exhausted me. The emotion, the physical demands I was making on my body: everything. Regardless of these feelings, I was thrilled that St. John's was hosting a benefit event for me. I was eager and honored to attend.

St. John's is very dear to my heart. So many of my closest friends and fondest memories come from this place. I was lucky enough to learn how to live the right kind of life there. It felt wonderful to return at this challenging point in my life. It gave me strength.

DAY 110

TUESDAY, SEPTEMBER 23, 2008

TODD: 9:12 PM

Hi everyone!

I hope you are all doing well.

It has been a busy few days since I last wrote. My rehab has been wearing me out and I have been falling asleep earlier.

I want to thank the great people from SJU and St. Joe for the wonderful benefit last Saturday. They hosted a tailgate party before the game and a party at LaPlayette after the game.

At halftime they said some very kind words and introduced me to the crowd. I was lucky to hear many cheers during my playing days, but never had one as heartfelt as that one. It is a moment I will always remember. I am very grateful for that memory. St. John's has always been a special place for me.

It has been interesting these past few days as I am starting to heal faster. I find myself remembering more of the day of the accident and the early days in the hospital.

Tonight Erica showed me some pictures of my first few days in ICU. It was hard to look at, but it also makes me grateful for the recovery I have had.

Today I met with my orthopedic surgeon, Dr. Morgan, who performed the pelvic and spinal surgery. He was very pleased with how the bones were healing and that things were looking good.

It was a little surreal to meet with him because I saw him primarily in the first few weeks of the accident. I was pretty out of it then. I found myself studying his face as he spoke to me. I was trying to remember our meetings before.

It is a very powerful and humbling thing, meeting with someone who helped to save your life and put your body back together.

> It is a very powerful and humbling thing, meeting with someone who helped to save your life and put your body back together.

I told him, as I told Dr. Ly, that there is not a day that passes that I do not think of him and the great work he did on me. And that I am grateful for him each day.

I could see in his eyes that he felt the emotion in my voice and the sincerity in my eyes. He said, "That means a great deal to me, thank you." As he left the room and I turned to my nurse, she fought back the same tears Dr. Ly's nurse did two weeks ago.

I could have just said, "Thanks Doc" as I left the room, but it would not have carried what needed to be said. It would not have justified the moment and how grateful I was to be here.

Today I saw pride in both of their faces, and that made me feel good.

It is so very important in this fast-paced world that we always remember that a thank you should be delivered slowly, with sincere eye contact and personal gratitude.

And, as it is in life, the giving is always the gift.

God bless you,

Todd

GUESTBOOK:

My family and I just begun listening to some CDs from the library called One Month To Live. *So many of the things shared on these remind me of thoughts you have shared on your CaringBridge site about what is really important in life!*

Thanks for your words of encouragement as you fight to regain the ability to walk again. Keep up the great work. May God give you strength each day!

Livija Ford

LOOKING BACK...

Expressing gratitude and appreciation is so important. When we go to the doctor, we often just think that this professional sitting before us is obligated to help. We look at these people as if they've got all the answers and can "fix us." In fact, we demand that they do. But here's something to remember: we can only wish within reason.

I realized that my doctors are just as human as I am. They need to hear my gratitude expressed for their work in the same way I would thank any of my workers for a job well done. These doctors and I were so connected. The work that they did for me—I can't even comprehend that complexity. They did this incredible service of repairing my body so that I could continue living my life.

When I thanked Doctor Ly and Doctor Morgan, I could see the impact my words made. They looked at me with kindness and warmth. It's not enough to assume that gratitude is known. We should express what we're feeling.

DAY 113

FRIDAY, SEPTEMBER 26, 2008

TODD: 11:39 PM

Hello my dear friends,

I have spent so much time talking about me I sometimes forget to ask you how you are doing.

So how goes life for you? I hope you are finding the greatness in each day and the opportunity of the next.

It has been a good week for me. I had one bad day yesterday but recovered nicely today. I have been lucky this past month with mostly great days.

My rehab went well this week. My land rehab included a lot of stretching and bar work. I was able to walk well on the bars and they moved me up to a walker! I have walked with the walker about fifty steps so far. It is very exciting.

My pool work also went very well. I was able to take about ten steps in the three-foot depth yesterday. I was a little shaky but did not fall over. I hope to try a few steps without the bars or walker within the next few weeks! We will see.

The pool is my favorite workout as it is less stress on my body. I have had two workouts so far, but this last one kind of hit home. I found myself humbled by the experience as I noticed the challenges the others face in the pool.

Once again I feel very lucky. I'm grateful for the opportunity to get better and see progress each time, but I'm humbled by the courage and determination of those around me. I think of their challenges each day and the things we take for granted.

This week I met a man who I watched walk in the pool the first day I was there. He looked about my age. I watched him slowly and awkwardly walk down the long ramp into the pool.

I remember thinking I want to be like him!

I thought he was probably a few months ahead of me in rehab. As I went to the pool for my workout yesterday I saw him wheeling past me toward the locker room, so I stopped him and introduced myself. I told him I wanted to walk like him and that he inspired me that day. As we talked he gave me some good advice on rehab and daily life. He told me that life was, of course, challenging—but it's also great. We have it. It's ours.

What a gift.

I asked him how long ago he had his accident and he said four-and-a-half years ago!

We talked some more and he told me about how well he was doing and how grateful he was. I can't help but think that his encouragement helped me have a great day in the pool.

He is like most of the people I meet at the Courage Center. They all smile and have a gratefulness about them.

I hope we are all so lucky.

God's blessings,

Todd

GUESTBOOK:

Dear Todd and family,

I have to say, every time I read your messages, I am encouraged in my daily walk.

God bless you as you continue with your rehab. You definitely are a blessing to many.

Sincerely,

Jean Spong

LOOKING BACK...

I have a vivid memory from the Courage Center. When I first arrived, I noticed a man making his way into the swimming pool. He was walking down the ramp into the water. Though he was struggling, he made it on his own. As I sat there in my wheelchair watching the man, I thought I want to walk like him.

DAY 115

TODD: 10:36 PM

Hi everyone,

Today, September 28, is a special day for me. It is my birthday, but it carried more meaning this year.

You see, today was the date that I set to walk again. I kept this goal to myself. I didn't even tell Erica. I would think of this day often in the hospital and was excited when it finally arrived.

I woke up today with the hope that I would find the energy and the right moment to try. I understood that it might not happen and I was OK with that.

Late this afternoon I decided to give it a try and, in front of my family, I was able to walk a few steps without my walker. It felt amazing and my kids went nuts! It was a moment I will always remember. I hope to get rid of these ortho boots and walk in tennis shoes soon.

Thanks again for all of your support!

God bless,

Todd

GUESTBOOK:

Todd,

How great to see you out and about this weekend! I had no idea it was your birthday today: so glad it was such a happy one for you. I'm continually amazed by you, and that family of yours.

Thank you for sharing your experience with all of us. You have touched the lives of many, many people through all your journal entries with your open and honest heart. Kai prayed again for "Timmy's dad" tonight. We'll keep the prayers coming in hopes that you will gain strength daily and be walking in your tennis shoes soon. Congratulations on those first steps without the walker . . . that is just wonderful!

Blessings,

Martha and Judd Sather

———

Happy birthday Fultzy!

As you know, it was homecoming at St. John's this past weekend and many thoughts were with you and your family. I do have to confess there were a few laughs at your expense, but I know next year you'll be there to defend yourself. My guess is you'll probably be tearing up the dance floor at Sal's during homecoming of '09!

I'll DJ.

Kalk (Jon Kalkbrenner)

LOOKING BACK...

Mary, my oldest daughter, had to process the trauma of seeing me at the hospital that summer. I wanted to trump that memory by giving her something positive to remember from this ordeal instead of something scary.

I managed to get up the stairs in our house without anyone knowing about it except my dad. It was the first time I had challenged the stairs, and in order to do so, I had to go up step by step on my butt, using my arms to move me. It was grueling, but I was determined to make this happen. He had my walker waiting on the landing at the top. From there I made my way into Mary's bedroom. I had grandpa tell her to run upstairs and turn off her TV. Meanwhile I would be waiting there for her—ready to show off some of my first steps.

There was no inkling among my family members that I could make it to the second floor of our house. When Mary ran into her room, she sensed someone in her periphery, and there I was, sitting on a chair reading a book nonchalantly. Shocked and smiling, she flew downstairs announcing that Dad was upstairs in her room!

The family came racing up to find me, and there, in Mary's bedroom, I made some of my first steps without my walker. I'm hoping this memory is the one my daughter holds closest when she remembers her dad's recovery.

DAY 121

FRIDAY, OCTOBER 3, 2008

TODD: 9:55 AM

Hi everyone,

What a great fall day today is. I have already been outside to enjoy it.

The leaves are a little brighter and the smells a little stronger this year. I find myself just stuck in the moment many times now. I am very grateful to be here.

This has been a wonderful week for little victories. You may remember my story about the shots I had to give myself each day—well, about 110 shots later, I am done. It was a great relief. I am also off my painkillers, which is good.

My rehab has also been going great with many little victories. On Thursday I took 120 steps in a row with my walker. And, based on my improvement, they will be moving my rehab up to five days a week! This is very exciting as I will see a little more improvement each day.

As I sat down to write this morning I found myself looking out our kitchen window at my neighbor's driveway. Their house is set back and we can't see it from ours.

What we do see is their driveway, gray gravel that travels along with green grass on both sides. There is a white fence with many tall trees that climbs a small hill and disappears into the forest. The morning sun hit it just right and left a warm feeling as it shot through the branches. It was a very comforting view. As I watched it I thought of the road I had traveled these past four months.

It made me think of all the beauty along the way. And yet, even with all that beauty, we face an uncertain destination over each hill: some will be good and some bad. But each day brings new travels and new opportunities. And, as long as you stay on the road, no matter how many bumps or how many hills, you will make it.

I sure appreciate each day and each opportunity and I hope you are able to do the same.

God's blessings to you!

Todd

GUESTBOOK:

Todd, Erica, Mary, Tim, and Madeline,

What a pleasure to read your short essay about what you experienced this morning. As I tried to express in the few times Alice and I have visited, I admire your courage and drive to lick this downturn in your life. It shows in the wonderfully philosophical writing that you do. Keep it up and God bless you and your family.

Now just a bit about my life for the past few days. Just before Alice and I moved from Crookston, I started working the sugar beet harvest for a farmer there. I have returned each year since and this year was no different.

My job is to drive a truck for the midnight to noon shift. That involves driving 100 - 250 miles during that time and hauling something like 10-20 loads of 14-15 tons per load to the pile where the beets are stored. Each night this year the stars have been absolutely brilliant. Sometimes a meteorite traces a path across the sky.

Because of your courage and willingness to tell about your struggles and successes, I take special delight in seeing each of these sunrises. God will give us as many as is right for me or you.

But the best comes as the night begins to fade and the eastern sky begins to turn color. It ends after a kaleidoscope, with the orange ball of the sun and the crisp-blue sky.

Because of your courage and willingness to tell about your struggles and successes, I take special delight in seeing each of these sunrises. God will give us as many as is right for me or you.

Thanks for you my nephew,
Paul Holm

LOOKING BACK...

Looking out the window on that fall morning, I saw a framed landscape that struck me as symbolic of the road I traveled to get here. The driveway, bending under the trees. The sun rising in the distance. This image resonated with me.

This morning gave me a chance to reflect on how far I had come, and reminded me of the long journey ahead. There's a lot of beauty along the way if I choose to see it. What lay before me out that window was a scene to be appreciated.

It's crucial to take the time to notice these simple things. Slow down. Live those moments of stillness. I drive down the road at the end of a long day and I see a stunning sunset. I watch while the other cars I pass drive hurriedly onward, and I think how we ought to, all of us, be pulling over onto the side of the road taking this in.

DAY 131

MONDAY, OCTOBER 13, 2008

TODD: 10:20 PM

Hi everyone!

Life is going great here. I have been working hard on rehab with three days in the pool and two days on land. I am taking about 150 steps a day with my walker. I am working on walking correctly and standing tall.

I had a special day last Saturday as our family went to the fire station open house in Stillwater as we do each year. They have tons of stuff for the kids and it is a great time.

This year meant a little more though. Within minutes of arriving at the event I was greeted by Fire Chief Stuart Glaser. He had a big smile and said how glad he was to see me. He and his crew were one of the first on the scene of my accident. I am so grateful for them.

It was a special moment to introduce my family to Stuart and thank him and his staff for all they did.

As you can see by the photo I got up enough energy to stand up.

I have been blessed to have so many wonderful people share their talents, their prayers, and their love with me in so many special ways.

I am thankful for all of you!

God bless,

Todd

GUESTBOOK:

Rock on! What a great picture to celebrate life!

How incredible it must be for the firefighters to be witness to such an inspirational story. We're so thrilled for you, Todd, and your whole remarkable family!

God bless,

Amy Karlstad

LOOKING BACK...

I had the chance to see the firemen who helped me the day of the accident. I thanked them wholeheartedly and let them know how busy I was as of late. I was very engaged in my rehab, and it felt good to be progressing.

DAY 142

FRIDAY, OCTOBER 24, 2008

TODD: 10:25 PM

Hi everyone!

Sorry for the delay in entries, it has been busy. Since I last wrote I went fishing, had a great doctor's appointment, and moved.

OK, the big one first: I went fishing and had a great time. Caught some crappies and bass. It was a beautiful night. Fishing has always been an important part of my life and it was really rewarding to be back on the water again. The picture on the welcome page was the first fish I caught on Monday night!

We also moved to the other side of Stillwater this week. The floor plan is better and we have a lot more room. There is a main floor bedroom with a private bath, so I am able to sleep in our bed again! It is nice to feel like things are getting back to normal a little.

Erica's father, David, bought the house with us. It is nice to have the extra adult around to help out.

I met with Doctor Ly this week and he gave me a good report. Everything is healing on schedule and I am now able to wear normal shoes with ankle supports. This is huge! I am very excited about it. I tried on a pair of socks for the first time yesterday and then put on my winter boots. I wanted to wear something else, but the boots were the only ones that fit, as my right foot is still swollen. I wore the boots for a few hours and then took them off. It is scary to walk without the constant support of my ortho boots.

I am now splitting time between my wheelchair and walker, but hope to be done with the wheelchair soon. I am going to try and take a few steps in normal shoes and without my walker in the next week or so.

Rehab is still going well. I am getting stronger each time and see little improvements. I still ice about three times a day. I am very lucky to have the Courage Center here in Stillwater.

I hope things are going well for you. It was sure a beautiful fall this year. I truly enjoyed seeing it, hope you did too.

God bless,
Todd

GUESTBOOK:

Wow—what a nice surprise this morning as I log in to see you holding a fish! You are unbelievable. You definitely have inspired us each day.

I see Erica now and then dropping off/picking up your kids at LADC. At the rate of your recovery, it won't be long before we see you there again! I also need to thank you as you have helped me through some difficult times with your philosophical journal entries.

God bless you and your family,
Heidi Koenig

———

Todd,
Bobber down and spirits up! Good to hear you're doing well and progressing in your recovery. The Johnnies squeaked another one out in Northfield Saturday. Blessings abound!
Dusty SJU
Michael Wagner

LOOKING BACK...

Going fishing? Sounds great.

When I accepted the offer, I knew I had a real challenge ahead of me—or I should say, below me. Going on this trip meant descending the stairs from the bluff down to the water. I was forced to shimmy down the seventy steps on my butt using my arms to push me. That descent took me fifteen minutes. Once I made it to the boat, however, I realized how worthwhile that struggle was.

I remember floating out on that placid lake with my buddies. Sitting there in that boat with a line and a lure lifted my spirits enough to climb back up those stairs and finish the week. I could have refused this offer to go fishing, but I didn't. I dealt with the discomfort, and I am so happy I did so.

DAY 148

THURSDAY, OCTOBER 30, 2008

TODD: 9:25 AM

Hello everyone!

Things are going well. Rehab is great and I am seeing progress each time.

I have been given the blessing by my doctor to start wearing shoes again with ankle supports. It is great to get away from those heavy ortho boots. It took a couple of days but I found some extra-wide work boots that I can get my foot in. It is still swollen and a little hard to get in, but it's worth it.

I am working to transition out of my wheelchair by using my walker as much as possible. Each time I do I am developing more strength and mobility. I hope to be done with the wheelchair by Thanksgiving.

I am very grateful for every little victory. Each one takes me one step closer.

As we have all found out, life keeps going despite the challenges and changes we face. We are blessed with the opportunity to face each day and decide what we want to get from it.

Wish me well as I leave in a few minutes to head to Sundance, Wyoming to go on our annual deer hunting trip with my father. We have two doctors in our group and an ATV for me, so I will be ok. I will be back on Tuesday night with an update.

We only get so many hunting trips with Dad in our lifetime. I just can't sit and watch one go by. I have to seize this moment. I hope you can find one to seize too!

God bless,

Todd

GUESTBOOK:

Todd,

Your recovery is phenomenal and truly blessed. Good luck on your hunting trip with Dad. I noticed you will be in Wyoming, so don't get too close to the Cheney ranch when you are hunting. He might still be in D.C. until Tuesday however.

Good luck and good hunting,
Jerry Fellows

LOOKING BACK...

I asked my doctors if I could go on a hunting trip with my dad and our buddies. Well, OK, I told them I was going. I knew I had to go, if only to defend my biggest buck title of the last five years. My doctors smirked at me. They knew there was no changing my mind.

This deer hunting trip is more about fellowship than anything else. It's a created event that turned into a tradition, and it became a tradition that brought people together.

As a kid, I remember going out to the garage after my dad would return from a deer hunting trip, and I would find an enormous buck. It impressed me and I knew I wanted to participate in this tradition myself one day. The idea of missing even one year of this tradition with my dad was unfathomable. I knew I was going to Wyoming with the guys.

> This deer hunting trip is more about fellowship than anything else. It's a created event that turned into a tradition, and it became a tradition that brought people together.

The decision to go ahead on this trip serves as an example of me controlling my own life—making my own decisions—instead of life and disability controlling me. I wasn't going to let this injury change how I lived my life.

I managed to return home with a six point buck on that trip. Everything from shooting the deer to having my picture taken with was challenging, but I didn't want to change this trip that I looked forward to every year if I could help it. I fought through the discomfort, and enjoyed the victories that came along with the battle.

DAY 159

WEDNESDAY, NOVEMBER 12, 2008

TODD: 7:07 PM

Hello everyone,

I am walking!

It isn't pretty and only about twelve steps, but I did it without any assistance! I have waited for this day a long time. I know you have too. It is here, and it happened, and I am truly grateful.

I will still need to use my walker most of the time, but it won't be long before that is gone too.

I promised everyone a "walking party" when I am able to walk again, and I will deliver. With the holidays coming I will plan on booking it for January—a great way for us to kick off the new year. It will be my treat and my way of saying thank you to each of you face to face. Hopefully, I will be walking completely on my own by then.

Today was a big victory in a long line of little victories. I am so excited and grateful for your support over these past five months. Your words and prayers have carried me through some difficult times, and inspired me to accomplish these first few steps.

It is hard to believe that this day has arrived, as I can still feel the impact of the crash. But as powerful as that impact was on June 5, the effect of 32,606 visits to the CaringBridge site, the thousands of prayers, letters, e-mails, phone calls, and personal visits and your overwhelming belief and spirit have given us this victory. Thank you so much!

As I said at one of the benefits, "It takes a village to heal a child." Well, this kid is walking—nice work village.

God bless,
Todd

GUESTBOOK:

Todd,

I know you must have traveled through some valleys, but you kept your sights on the mountain top and you did it! My prayers continue for your continued strength and your family's good health.

Joyce Kisch

Todd,

Yes, it takes a village, but it also takes courage, determination and an astounding faith on your part. Keep working kid—great things are happening!

God bless,

Sue Gort

LOOKING BACK...

The timing was perfect. I told everyone that I wanted to try something, and I walked across an open space, from one corner of the room to the other. It felt like a huge leap.

This day felt like the end of one chapter and the start of a new one. This was my pinnacle. I was expecting smooth sailing from here.

DAY 166

TODD: 9:57 PM

Hello everyone!

I hope you and your family are well.

Things are going great here. Each week more little victories.

I received the OK to start driving again. What a blessing. The freedom that driving provides is such a gift—it has really helped me feel more like I was before the accident. I throw my walker in the truck and off I go. It is great. I even drove Mary to school the other day. That was a lot of fun.

I recently made another little victory: stairs. I am able, with the help of the wall and railing, to get up and down stairs. It is slow going but well worth it.

This is huge because our children's bedrooms are upstairs and I am now able to go up to tuck them in. It is so great to spend that time with them, a time I missed dearly these past five months.

Last night, I had one of those great "daddy moments" with my son, Tim. Every night the last thing I say to each of the kids is "I am so glad you are my son (or daughter)."

Last night after five-year-old Tim and I talked for a while, I tucked him in and said goodnight. I then looked him in the eye and smiled and said, "Timmy, I am so glad you are my son."

Tim replied, "Dad, you have said that to me 10,000 times!"

I said, "I just want you to know that I love you."

And Tim said, "Dad, I can tell that by your smile when you say that to me."

I am so grateful to have had the opportunity to tuck our children in again. But it is even better to know that they know I love them. I will always remember that moment.

There are many blessings in each day if we just slow down and take the time to see them and appreciate them. I hope you are taking a moment to enjoy your blessings as well.

God bless you tonight!

Todd

GUESTBOOK:

Awesome! Congratulations! Yet it is not surprising. You have created this moment through focus, determination, and hope. Yes, I don't think we can tell our kids enough how we feel about them. Sounds like you're also a powerful demonstrator of good fathering.

Mike Wenzel

———

Todd,

You don't actually know me, but I am from Stillwater originally and I graduated from high school with Erica. My name is Keri (Mears) Kaboushek. I am sorry to say that I just recently learned of your horrific accident.

Since then I have read your entire site, every journal entry. I had planned to check out the site for the gist of how you are doing and what exactly happened, but I couldn't stop reading. I cried, I laughed, and I felt so inspired by both you and Erica. You are an amazing man, husband, and father. You have come a long way and are truly a blessing and a miracle. Keep up the good work and may God bless you and your beautiful family.

Have a wonderful Thanksgiving! I will be checking your site regularly to follow on your progress.

Take care and God bless!

Keri (Mears) Kuboushek

LOOKING BACK...

It was such a novel experience, going up stairs. A totally new world was opened up to me. This part of our new house was foreign to me, so to climb those stairs—to see furniture and objects I recognized in my children's bedrooms—was a rush of nostalgia and comfort.

I guided myself up those stairs slowly. I knew then that if my kids needed me for something, I would be able to meet them at the top.

It's strange to live on a property, but only participate in a portion of it. I was missing out on an entire realm of my house. Getting up those stairs meant opening a door in my recovery.

DAY 178

TODD: 10:39 PM

Hello everyone,

Thank you for the many kind words. You have guided me through so much these past six months with your encouragement and prayers.

This has been a special Thanksgiving for us. I truly appreciated the weekend and seeing so many friends and family. I am very grateful for that opportunity.

I scored another little victory today as I was able to trade in my walker for two canes. This is the last step to "walking free," and it felt really good. I am able to stand up straighter and get in a better walking motion with the canes. Plus, I can now fend off any attackers like a ninja!

> What is important is simply the time we spend with our family and friends. Things change fast in this life, so focus on your time. . .you will never regret it.

I go in for a CAT scan tomorrow and meet with Dr. Morgan on my pelvis and spine at the end of the month.

My rehabs have been going great and my flexibility is coming back. I am starting to find more freedoms in my life and continue to be humbled to have that opportunity each day.

I know this holiday season is here and the times are going to get a little crazy for everyone, but just remember that it is the times that are the most important. It's not the turkey or the presents, not the egg nog or the tree or anything else that we seem to get so concerned about. What is important is simply the time we spend with our family and friends. Things change fast in this life, so focus on your time . . . you will never regret it.

May God bless you and keep you,
Todd

GUESTBOOK:

Hey Todd,

I have been meaning to drop you a line after I saw you and Erica the other night. It was so great to see you out and walking around. Now you have made another great stride to recovery: you give so many of us inspiration to focus on our daily lives, cherishing everything that we have and who we have to cherish it with.

I look forward to the day that I see you two out again!

Heidi Koenig

LOOKING BACK...

Using the canes to move was another step and made me so excited. I think I started crying. It was another little victory in a long line of steps that amounted to one big goal. I was feeling optimistic on this day.

DAY 184

SUNDAY, DECEMBER 7, 2008

TODD: 10:01 PM

Hello everyone,

I hope you are well.

It has been a good week, as today I was able to wear tennis shoes for the first time in six months. It was great: much easier to get around. I normally wear size ten and a half but now I wear size thirteen so my right foot will fit. My foot is still swollen, and that swelling may be there for a while. The footwear makes it much easier to get up and down the stairs and to walk around with my canes.

It was challenging outside this weekend with the snow. It slows everything down and I have to watch and focus on every step. Even when I come inside I have to be careful that my shoes and canes are not wet or I slip easily. I now understand why people go south for the winter: they don't want to fall. I guess I won't be too far behind them.

I scored a little victory on Thursday at the Courage Center as I was able to walk into the pool for the first time. Before I needed a wheelchair and the ramp to enter, but now I use my canes and walk down the steps. It was a powerful moment as I thought about the first day I had pool therapy back in September and I watched a guy about my age struggle to walk into the pool. I said that day that I wanted to walk like him, and Thursday I did.

Thursday night I had a scare when I had some internal issues around 10:00. I felt an "adjustment" inside my chest, like things dropped and shifted. I looked in the mirror and had a bulge sticking out of my stomach a few inches above my belly button.

Erica took me to the emergency room and the doctor said it was a surgical hernia. It happens often after surgery when the incision does not hold completely. It is not a big deal on the medical side, but on the personal side it does not go away and I will carry this bulge around with me for the rest of my life. It was a little scary but I am glad it was nothing serious.

> I felt an "adjustment" inside my chest, like things dropped and shifted. I looked in the mirror and had a bulge sticking out of my stomach a few inches above my belly button.

You know, we all have things about us that may not look right or that we are unhappy with. There are many people who judge us for what we have or don't have or how we look, or walk, or talk. God judges us only by who we are and how we treat people, how we help those less fortunate. Do we cast stones or do we heal the sick? Do we take advantage of the weak, or do we share a few fishes and loaves of bread so hundreds can eat?

Our ability to spread God's grace is not based solely on how much you believe in God, but how much you believe in yourself, because the belief in yourself is an extension of your faith in God. It is that belief in self that ignites God's grace within you and inspires you and guides you as you share it with others. You have many gifts to share and many people to inspire, to help, and to love.

And, as you will find, the gifts you share will pale in comparison to the gifts you receive by sharing God's grace.

I am very grateful to spend this Christmas and holiday season with all of you. Thank you again for helping to get me here.

God bless you,

Todd

GUESTBOOK:

Todd,

Your enormous challenge is upheld so nicely by your optimism and honesty. We don't know each other all that well, but your authenticity through this is really touching and moving. I have grown reading your journal entries and am keeping you and your family in our prayers. God bless: keep up the hard work and may God be with you as you move from victory to victory by way of a setback or two.

Peace,

Will Berigan and family

———

Hi Todd and family,

It's so great to hear the news and read about your amazing journey. You are such an inspiration to us and I have learned so much more about my friend in the past six months that I will cherish the rest of my life.

May the holidays be extra special for you this year and may God continue to work his magic.

Love and warm wishes your way,

Greg and Lynn Kienholz

LOOKING BACK...

It felt as if the stairs I was climbing toward recovery had disintegrated underfoot. I was terrified.

Erica and I sped off to the emergency room and faced more uncertainty and confusion in the hospital. I was still floating on the positive achievements I had made in the previous weeks, so I was not as afraid as I would have been had I known what was in store for me.

I felt close to God.

DAY 195

THURSDAY, DECEMBER 18, 2008

ERICA: 2:13 PM

Hello everyone! Happy holidays to you all.

We have moved to another house in Stillwater. It is very nice because it has a main floor bedroom, so Todd is no longer on display in the TV room. Everyone is adjusting beautifully. Just say some prayers for the sale of our old house.

I hope you all enjoy these days leading up to Christmas. Love to you all!

Erica

GUESTBOOK:

Todd,

You are now very close to us as we are on the other side of the Stillwater High School from you. Glad to hear that you are doing well and making great strides in your recovery. Keep it up.

Merry Christmas,

Korey Finnes

Thanks for stopping in and seeing me at work—it was great to see your smiling face! You and your family have a merry Christmas.

Mike Gannon

LOOKING BACK...

Worry consumed me. I didn't know how to feel about this hernia ordeal in my stomach. I felt as low as I had felt in a really long time. The clouds of disappointment were closing in. This internal drama was something that we couldn't just stretch some duct tape over. This was serious.

Along with that hernia came some pretty deep fears and depression. I saw how attitudes can be contagious.

I was incapable of writing during this month, so Erica did my journal entries for me.

Along with that hernia came some pretty deep fears and depression. I saw how attitudes can be contagious. I saw how my mood was affecting my family. I knew I wanted to keep my spirits up, but this new visit to the hospital was a surprise and a severe struggle.

DAY 209

THURSDAY, JANUARY 1, 2009

TODD: 11:02 PM

Hello everyone!

Hope your holiday was wonderful. We had a great one.

Rehab is going well as I continue to gain strength and stability. Walking outside is challenging as I have to watch each step and prepare for a safe route to my destination. Everything is slower, but slowing down helps you appreciate things a little more.

A few weeks back I mentioned I had an incisional hernia and that they were not going to do anything about it. After meeting with my surgeon at Regions they decided to fix it, so Friday morning I am going in for a quick little surgery to repair it. I should only be in the hospital for a day or two. After that, look out: I will be ready to go!

I have been blessed by your prayers throughout this process and I am grateful for them. Tomorrow, if you could, please include my dear friends David Doyscher and Geraldine Seeley in your prayers as well. Please ask for God's blessings for them.

I hope you are well and finding the beauty in each day. It is really such a blessing to be here and to grasp the opportunity of each day. It is amazing what we can accomplish, what we are capable of and how we can take God's inspiration and share it with others.

God bless you this New Year as you share that inspiration.

Todd

GUESTBOOK:

So glad to hear your rehab is progressing. Bill tried to call you during the holidays and said he had to leave you a message. We just wanted to let you know that we were thinking of you guys and hoping your holidays were going well.

Good luck with your surgery this am. Will watch for an update after the surgery.

Wishing you a blessed 2009!

Judy and Bill Mansun

LOOKING BACK...

As family friends began to go through their own strife, I was put to the ultimate test. How does one deal with these dark valleys in life? A Minnesota winter doesn't help with the internal drama, and my energy stores were at an all-time low for this new year's challenges.

I had friends at Regions Hospital, but I wasn't prepared to see them in this way. It's never easy going under for surgery, and this one snuck up on me. I was falling. I was afraid and I didn't know how far I would fall before that fear dispersed.

I dove back into the unknown in those hospital beds. I had no choice.

The doctors were supposed to be fixing my incisional hernia by inserting a kind of netting around my stomach. This seemed like a great way to fix the problem, but there was a catch. If for some reason the net broke or just didn't hold, the doctors wouldn't be able to put the same netting product back inside me. This caused a lot of concern in the faces of my doctors. Although this was a solution in the moment, it might be a problem down the road.

In that moment, I saw more drugs and more healing, another steep hill I would need to climb. Even though I was tired from all the climbing I had done over the summer and fall—even though I was worried and confused—I dove back into the unknown in those hospital beds. I had no choice.

DAY 210

ERICA: 8:31 PM

Hello everyone,

Wow, I felt like I stepped back in time today. It was not so pleasant, let me tell you. While Regions is a fabulous hospital, it really isn't a place that I like to spend much time. Todd's doctor spent about two and a half hours in surgery. He originally wanted to do a laparoscopic procedure, but it seems Todd's belly was a bit more challenging. As the doctor put it, "He was quite a mess." They have such nice ways of putting things. His other doctor calls Todd his "favorite train wreck."

Anyway, they ended up putting a mesh liner on the entire abdominal wall. The doctor feels like there is an increased risk for infection because he was thinking there was infection already in Todd's stomach. Let's pray really hard that he steers clear of any infection, because they would have to take that entire mesh out. Todd is in significant pain—he is having a hard time managing it right now. He is so tough though, I am sure he will be better in the morning.

Thank you all for your prayers. I anticipate him being in the hospital for about three to four days while they do all they can to prevent infection. Of course, the kids are getting sick.

Again, thank you for your prayers for our friends, we love them so.

I'll keep you updated! Just fine in '09, right?

Love,

Erica

GUESTBOOK:

Hang in there sweetie. We are praying for Todd's quick recovery, no infection, health for the kids, and for patience and sanity for you.
Love you lots,
Zanny Johnson

———

Hi Todd, Erica, Mary, Tim, and Madeline,
It is now 8:30 am in Iringa, about 11:30 pm in Minnesota. However, it is now January 3rd for us while you are approaching the end of January 2nd.

We are pleased to know that the surgery is over and you are now dealing with recovery. Pain for sure, but hopefully that can and will be managed in an acceptable way.

With the presence of an abscess already, it is most fortunate that the surgery was performed in order to address the presence of infection sooner rather than later.

We pray for the antibiotic to do its good work and for your body to be given the strength to assist in the battle of reducing and eliminating the infection.

We are doing well in Iringa and are getting settled into our role of welcoming guests which starts already this next week. Sunday we will go to Ifuwa with Chris, Heidi, Gary, and an interpreter. It looks like Don will be the preacher.

Thanks be to God for successful surgery and now prayers for infection control will ascend. Again, the strong positive attitude and fighting spirit will assist the powerful work of medicine: in combination we have a winner.

Peace and blessings,
Don and Eunice Fultz

LOOKING BACK...

You enter into surgery blindly—it's the only way.

I came out of this hernia surgery with extreme pain in my back and stomach. Learning to deal with a new pain and seeking out new comfort zones to alleviate that pain was a great challenge.

This road felt uncertain, scarred with potholes and obstacles. Instead of confidence, I felt fear and apprehension. Erica sensed my emotions and followed me nervously as we took this new fork in the road that led to the darkest part of our journey together.

DAY 213

MONDAY, JANUARY 5, 2009

ERICA: 10:43 PM

Hello all! I hope you are all doing great!

Just wanted to write a quick update. Todd is still at Regions. His body just takes a little more time to bounce back these days, obviously. He is getting up a little more now, which is awesome. We are hoping he gets out on Thursday or Friday, cross your fingers.

He is still in a lot of pain, and is super tired.

I'll keep you updated.

Love,

Erica

GUESTBOOK:

Hi Todd,

Been watching your progress all fall. You are doing great! This latest operation is another hurdle you will clear and be right back on track.

Pheasant season is over for another year. I left a whole bunch for next year when you can join me. My two-year-old lab was absolutely fantastic. You will love hunting with her! Hang in there.

Steve Charron

LOOKING BACK...

I arrived at the hospital on a Friday, anticipating my return home the following Monday or Tuesday. Monday came and went, leaving me at the hospital, despondent and low.

I waited and waited for my levels. I waited all week.

The surgeons put a tube inside my stomach that came out near my beltline. This tube was emptying my stomach of excess blood from the surgery. The blood levels had to reach a specific level before the doctors would let me leave the hospital.

I waited and waited for my levels. I waited all week.

DAY 214

ERICA: 11:20 PM

Hi all, I have my nightly update for you.

No huge change today. Todd is doing some more physical therapy, taking walks to visit his cute nurse friends.

That is about it: other than that he still sleeps and is feeling pretty sick. The doctors are going to try different medicines to see if his body wakes up a little more. He is not super happy about how things have been going, but what can you do? I am hoping these other medicines will do the trick—it would be nice to have him home soon. I am praying he'll be home by the weekend.

I hope you had a great day! Thanks for your notes, I love reading them.

Erica

GUESTBOOK:

Erica,

I know it is hard seeing your husband in so much pain. You feel so helpless. Watching them sleep has a double blessing. One, you know they are experiencing little discomfort. The other is that they are not getting enough activity to help them gain strength.

Have faith in God that He knows what is best for Todd. I am also praying for the wisdom of Todd's doctors to help Todd improve and return home.

Our daughter, Heidi Koenig, has told of us Todd. She also sent us this website.

In friendship,
Marlene Burkhalter

———

Hey Todd,

It was nice to meet you downstairs in rehab. Thanks for the vote of confidence!

Keep going strong. You made me see that it can be done if you work hard at it. Wish we had more time to get to know you. Take care and good luck. I thought we had a lot of hits on our website, but you are really kicking Britney Spears' butt! Keep them coming.

Paul and Terrie Kozey

LOOKING BACK...

The medical staff and I knew that I would be in the hospital ward longer than anticipated, so we made the best of it. I got to know my nurses and communicated as frequently as possible with my doctors.

Some of my nurses were from foreign countries. I recognized a few Tanzanian accents—sometimes I would surprise them when they'd take my vitals.

"Asante sana," I would say. This got the nurses excited. "You speak Swahili!" they would exclaim, eyes wide and disbelieving. I corrected them that I only spoke a little, but that was enough to make a few new connections with my caregivers.

I like meeting new people. Putting forth that extra effort to show you care will take you far in life.

DAY 221

ERICA: 10:41 AM

Good morning everyone! I have good news and bad news.

On Sunday, Todd was able to sweet talk to doctors into letting him come home. After he got home we had a nice dinner and hung out. In the middle of the night, however, he starting feeling sick.

When we woke up the next morning, I told him I felt like I had the flu. He told me the same.

We were both down and out when Todd called his doctor to give him an update. The doctor wanted Todd to come back to the hospital right away, to be sure he wasn't dehydrated. Unfortunately he was, so they started an IV. After four hours they did a CAT scan. It showed a blockage in his small intestine, probably a complication from surgery.

They ended up putting a tube down his nose to extract the blockage. The tube will have to stay in for one to two weeks. If it doesn't stop draining after two weeks, they will have to operate again.

The tube is incredibly uncomfortable and Todd is miserable. Please pray that things progress as easily as possible for him. This time we're looking at a hospital stay that, in the best case is a week: worst case, we're looking at a month! Your prayers were answered before, please join together again, so we can get him home and healthy.

They're pounding the walleyes at the fish house: we've got to get him up there!

All my love,
Erica

GUESTBOOK:

Dear Todd and Erica,

My oh my, it was difficult to read your update. I just want things to improve for you every day, not go sideways and backwards! "Please dear God, grant healing to Todd and faith and courage to Erica and the family to fight this new battle." We are weak but He is strong.

Love,

David and Gena Doyscher

LOOKING BACK...

I'd been pressing my doctors to send me home. Finally they relented and I was allowed to leave the hospital. I was only home a matter of hours before I started to see the major consequences of this move.

Ultimately I returned to the hospital, terrified again. It seemed everyone was groping in the dark, trying to determine what was wrong with me. I shouldn't have gone home. Now that I was back at Regions, I was at more of a loss than ever as to what was the matter.

> It seemed everyone was groping in the dark, trying to determine what was wrong with me.

It's scary to deal with all the question marks in a situation like this. What's happening inside of me? How serious is this? I remember sitting doubled over in Regions waiting room for an eternity. I waited until I was hooked up to an IV. I met with several surgeons, and we discussed what would happen next.

The decision was worse than I could have imagined. The words NG tube will forever strike fear into my heart. This tube was inserted up into my nostril, then pushed down the back of my throat and into my stomach where it would retract the material there. In theory this would allow my intestine to correct its position. Just hearing how the tube would be inserted made me gag, but what choice did I have?

I was in misery. The worst part: I was playing a waiting game.

DAY 222

FRIDAY, JANUARY 14, 2009

TODD: 8:52 PM

Hello everyone, it's Todd,

Erica was able to bring up the laptop tonight so I could visit with you. I hope this note finds you well.

I am doing OK here at Regions. They are working on fixing an obstruction of some type in my small intestine. I have a tube running down my nose and into my stomach to help drain the area and shrink the intestine. It is very uncomfortable and painful.

It could be anywhere from another day to ten days. Since I was just here for ten days I am praying to get out of here. If they can't fix it by then they will look to do another surgery.

It is hard to be away from my family for so long, but I am grateful for everything Erica is able to do.

Thank you for all the great messages. I enjoy reading them as it is difficult to talk now.

I will update more tomorrow.

God bless you!

Todd

GUESTBOOK:

Hey Todd!

The thoughts and prayers continue and I know your gift of strong character, work ethic, and faith will continue to sustain you. I'm thinking of you.

Godspeed!

Regan Smith

Hi Todd,

I just wanted to drop you a line and say hello. You and your family are in my thoughts and prayers often. I'm sorry that you are experiencing setbacks. I wish I had some wise words of wisdom for you, but I don't. I did, however, run across this quote the other day:

"When you feel like giving up, remember why you held on so long in the first place."

You have a beautiful family and more friends than most people could ever dream of. They are all praying for you and wish that they could change places with you for a while so that you could rest. Hang in there.

God bless you.

Julie Sandstrom

LOOKING BACK...

There were very few entries in which I discussed the extent of my pain. The fact that I did so in this entry testifies to the agony I was going through. It was hard for me to sleep at night because I felt as if I was constantly choking or gagging. I wasn't eating because machines were feeding me intravenously, a very helpless feeling.

The most vivid thing I remember was my throat. The tube rubbed against the interior of my throat, and before long I was battling the worst sore throat of my life. A callous eventually formed, and the pain went away a little.

I couldn't imagine a greater mental and physical challenge.

I couldn't imagine a greater mental and physical challenge.

Something happened late that night that I didn't mention in

the CaringBridge log—one of the nurses at Regions helped me out when I really needed it. I had a colossal sneeze and my NG tube actually flew up out of my stomach and through my nose. I immediately felt relief, but that was short-lived.

I realized I would need to have the tube reinserted. The mere thought brought tears to my eyes, but this amazing nurse—who happened to be doing rounds in my room at the time—helped me along. She calmed me down and told me she'd done this procedure many times before.

She wasn't lying. I only felt ten percent of the pain I had felt when the tube was initially inserted. I thanked her, and I hope she understood the depths of my gratitude for making a difficult moment in the middle of night a little easier on me. As far as I'm concerned, this nurse ranks right up there with the all-time greats.

DAY 223

THURSDAY, JANUARY 15, 2009

ERICA: 9:36 PM

Good evening friends,

We just got back from visiting Todd. They moved him to his own room, which is so much better. He has a view out his window and own space. I feel so much better for him.

I can't tell you how he amazes me more every day. It doesn't seem possible. From Monday until Wednesday of this week I laid in my bed feeling sorry for myself, and how this is such an awful situation. Can you believe that, the audacity?

Meanwhile Todd is sitting in the hospital with a painful tube in his nose through his stomach and he just presses on. I'm telling you, he is nothing short of amazing. In some ways I feel like this is a little worse than when the accident happened. At least then I knew that he would wake up, he would walk again, and the healing was happening every day.

Now it's a waiting game. Waiting to see if his blockage will be cleared, waiting to see if they have to do surgery, waiting, waiting, waiting. I have never, ever seen him as thin as he is. Could you imagine not eating for five straight days, with the prospect of food a week away, or two, three, or four? They pump one nutrient in for every two that goes out. He doesn't even want to eat ice chips because that measures in his output.

I need everyone to hear me now more than ever! Please channel all your positive energy, your prayers, your love into this healing for Todd! We want him home. He wants to be home. I know that our prayers were answered before, we can do it again. He's our miracle man, let's do it again!

I love each and every one of you for loving him. Let's help him, let's get him home!

Give your spouse, loved one, child an extra squeeze tonight, and know how lucky you are to do so.

Goodnight,

Erica

GUESTBOOK:

Todd,

It inspires me time and again to see how God shines light into the toughest of situations. You and your family (and all your great friends) are that light!

I thank God for continuing to fill you with such hope and faith for your future which allows you to share your deep words and thoughts of encouragement with the rest of us. That pretty well describes the word "ministry" for me.

Bet you weren't planning on becoming a minister, huh? What's next, you preaching on a Sunday morning? (We kind of already had you doing that in the video). Hope to see you soon

Rest and healing to you,

Phil Kadidlo

LOOKING BACK...

I had hit a wall waiting for my body to respond to the treatment. Though I had been navigating a tumultuous recovery before, this new snare on the trail really tripped me up. More than any other part of my year post-crash, it was this obstacle that threatened to pin me down in a way I couldn't maneuver out of.

I became good at calming myself down, concentrating on breathing, and focusing my thoughts on a horizon line: anywhere but here.

My body was becoming emaciated and weak as the days passed. I saw my reflection in the mirror, and there was this gaunt face staring back at me. I looked pale and sick. When Erica would walk into my room, I saw an instantaneous flash of despair when she'd look at me: I just didn't resemble my healthy self from eight months prior.

> My body was becoming emaciated and weak as the days passed. I saw my reflection in the mirror, and there was this gaunt face staring back at me. I looked pale and sick.

I remember looking out the window, which faced eastward. I imagined myself leaving that hospital bed as soon as I could. I pictured the family's car driving down Highway 94 eastward.

Homeward.

DAY 225

TODD: 8:57 PM

Hello everyone,
I am doing a little better today. This one has been a challenge.
I have found strength and inspiration in your kind words. You have lifted my spirits on a number of occasions this week. Thank you.
I hope to have an update in the next few days.
Just wanted to let you know that I am doing OK and that I'm grateful for your prayers!
God bless,
Todd

> **I have found strength and inspiration in your kind words.**

GUESTBOOK:

OK, you can do this! You have shown through all your incredible wisdom, spirit, and strength in your words that you can do this!

You have sounded so much like your Dad in all your writings. I know, because he was my pastor and I knew you in our youth. You can do this and we are all praying so much for an easier recovery and for you to be home with your family. God is with you! Your angels are with you! So many prayers are with you. Rest, and get well.

God bless and watch over you,
Diana Urness and family

———

Hi Todd,

Just wanted to let you know that you and your family are in our thoughts and prayers. I can only imagine how tough this has been for all of you. I'm hoping that soon you'll make an entry that says you're going home and that you've conquered yet another obstacle in your journey.

I'll let St. Patrick's know to continue praying for you.

Keep fighting and stay strong,

Wendy Dernovsek

LOOKING BACK...

Reading the messages friends and family left for me on CaringBridge gave me so much strength. I remember this day in January. I was still waiting for a change to happen so perhaps I could go home. Waiting was hard, but I felt more resilient after reading the encouragement people sent me.

I cried as I read through the things my friends wrote to me. How does it come to this?

I felt so blessed that they were lifting me along as best they could.

DAY 227

TODD: 11:57 PM

Hello everyone,

I hope this finds you well.

I had a few little victories yesterday that are helping me improve my condition and hopefully get me home this weekend!

They took the tube that ran through my nose and down my throat out this morning. That was a huge relief!

They are going to start me on liquids tomorrow and hopefully solid food in the next few days. If I can keep it down they will release me. We are praying for that, as surgery is the next option.

> Each night I think of my kids and wife as I go to bed. I can't wait to be home again.

I've spent seventeen days here this month. Each night I think of my kids and wife as I go to bed. I can't wait to be home again.

Count your blessings each day and praise God for them.

God bless you!

Todd

GUESTBOOK:

Todd, Erica, Mary, Timmy, and Madeline,

A note from Africa! We are nine hours ahead of your Minnesota time and therefore it is 12:38 noontime in Iringa. We are so very pleased to hear the good news about your drainage tube and the start of liquids and then some solid food. We are praying that your body will allow this to be processed into energy and that you can keep everything down. The thought/hope of going home this weekend has to be a powerful incentive to allow the body to do its good work and strive to get back with family and friends.

We especially pray that everything will work for good and let all the body parts do the work they need to do to provide you with good comfort and good function. The time still calls for patience and perseverance so that you can fully heal. We are praying that the surgical option will not have to be exercised. It will be wonderful to get back to the home and be with family and friends in that friendly and comfortable setting. It will especially mean that trips to the hospital and back will not have to be made!

Continue to trust God and pray that the hospital folk are doing everything in their power to allow you to heal and that the Good Lord will let the current journey come to a good conclusion. Keep up the strong spirit and desire to heal and get well and let your faith continue to inspire you.

Blessings to you all for comfort, healing, and enjoyable days ahead. Love you all!

Dad and Mom from Iringa, Tanzania

LOOKING BACK...

The doctors continued to extend the forecast for my hospital stay. I began asking myself if there was an end in sight.

Please let my condition improve, please send me home, I prayed on Monday night as I considered the prospect of another week with a tube down my throat.

The staff at Regions had been encouraging me to do a lot of walking. Moving my body would expedite the healing, they said, and so I was aggressively walking the halls of the hospital. It was a little maddening because there really wasn't anywhere I could walk *to*. I just paced the hallways, hoping that each step was doing some good and helping my condition.

As often as I could, I would make a point of walking to the wing of the hospital where Amy worked. She was one of my favorite nurses at Regions. She understood my situation and did a great job of making sure all my needs were met. We were even able to have a little fun joking around together. Whenever I got the chance I tried to visit her. There were some upsides to returning to Regions after all, even though I had to look pretty hard to find them.

That evening, the doctors commented that they were already seeing an improvement in my condition. The next morning, improvements were dramatic, and my solicitations to have my NG tube removed were met with approval! This was an incredible relief. The end was in sight.

At this point, I felt like I had a little more control over my destiny.

DAY 229

TODD: 1:56 PM

Hello everyone!

Things are going well. I started on solid foods today and they are staying down. The doctors met with me last night and said that, if today and tomorrow go well, I can go home on Friday. Wow!

I can almost see the finish line on this one and it feels really good. This was a challenging time both mentally and physically.

I am grateful to my brother Tim who showed me almost twenty-five years ago how to fight and how to smile. Last week, Steve, one of my doctors, stopped in to say goodbye as he was moving to another hospital for the next six months. Before he left, he said that he was so impressed with my fortitude and ability to stay positive and smiling through this entire process. He said he sees injuries like mine break many people in here. I told him thanks, but I had a great teacher on life and that I was just following his lead.

I am grateful for all of your prayers, support and your messages. I am grateful to the many people who helped my family with meals, rides, and work around the house while I've been in here. It's a comforting feeling to know that your family is looked after when you can't be there.

It is exciting to think of getting out of here as there is so much life to live. I hope you are finding time to "live" the important things in your life too.

God bless you,

Todd

> I am grateful to my brother Tim who showed me almost twenty-five years ago how to fight and how to smile.

GUESTBOOK:

I have been away but have been catching up on your newest Regions encounter. I am excited to hear you are heading home, but sad to be missing you there as I am back at work Friday. Oh well, I hope not to see you there anymore anyway! Keep up the hard work.

Elizabeth Luzum

LOOKING BACK...

I started to feel like I could see the end of the tunnel. I felt better, and my doctor would be making a special trip to see me on this day because of my progress. There was hype and energy in the air: I could feel that my release from Regions was imminent.

My conversation with Doctor Morgan went well. He told me that I had done a great job of keeping my chin up over those last few days—something that was rare in patients who had to deal with so many obstacles. "You're the type of patient we love to have," he said.

Hearing this meant a lot to me. I was proud that the doctor was acknowledging the work I'd done, and I hoped that my work encouraged him, too.

Sitting in my own room alone, I had a lot of time for reflection. My thoughts often drifted to my younger brother, Tim. I thought of how many challenges he faced and overcame when he was alive. I remembered how much he taught me. I talked to him a lot in that hospital room, and I told him how glad I was to have him as my brother. Calling upon Tim, leaning on him during those darker days—this was instrumental in my recovery. I felt his presence and I felt his support.

DAY 230

TODD: 10:38 AM

Hello everyone!

Great news . . . I am outta here! I did so well the past few days they are releasing me at about 10:00 this morning.

It is so exciting to be going home. Thanks again for all your support. I will keep you updated.

I've got to go now, before they change their mind. See ya!

God bless,

Todd

GUESTBOOK:

Fultzer,

Super Bowl coming up and you wanted to watch it at home, that's why you pressed to get out of there! About time you got outta there pal, I was thinking maybe you were getting interested in becoming a doctor. You'd probably be good at that too . . .

Glad to see you are going home Todd, get healthy bud!

Prayers from Iraq, (a little dusty, but they work the same over here as they do in the snow!)

Jeff Imsdahl, Kirkuk

———————

Todd and Erica,

Please check out David Doyscher's CaringBridge site for the latest info on birth and death. Hillary's baby arrived today (3:45 am), but David has slipped down quite low though he is still holding on. Happy and sorrowful times at once for them.

We are doing fine in Iringa. Tomorrow we worship at Kihesa, Don preaching. Gary is at the Cathedral, also preaching.

Our January groups have all returned to Minnesota; we have two groups coming in February. Lots of visitors to the office on Tuesdays and Thursdays. We've been having nice weather: 60s in the morning, 80s during the day. Some rains have fallen, but we can still use more as some places are quite dry with others having ample rains. Ruaha Park is quite dry so they could use some rain.

We hope and pray your recovery continues in a positive mode as does your attitude and spirit for gaining greater independence and strength. Fun to read the many responses from friends and relatives. Aunt Alice continues to do well from her hip replacement; Uncle Jim has surgery on his knee and is doing well; Don Conn had both knees replaced and his rehab is painful but steady and he is doing well.

We'll continue to keep you posted, but all is well in Africa. We hope the same for you and the family in Stillwater.

Peace and blessings!

Dad and Mom

LOOKING BACK...

I wanted to give the best possible impression, to show them that I was well and ready to be released. I made sure my room was clean and my bags were packed. I got rid of my hospital gown and put on a pair of shorts and a T-shirt, anything to show the doctors I was ready to go home.

I told the doctor, "I am ready to go. Things are good here."

My work paid off: the doctors agreed to let me go home. I was ecstatic. I called Erica and said, "Get down here as fast as you can. The doctors are letting me go, and if you can't pick me up, I'm getting in a cab."

As I walked out those hospital doors with Erica, I remember breathing in the frosty January air with total happiness. I earned this.

I was finally on my road home.

DAY 248

TODD: 9:54 PM

Hello everyone,

Hope you are all well.

It has been great to be home with my family these past few weeks. We have had a wonderful time together catching up. I am grateful for this time as I will be heading back to Regions in about a month for another surgery, this time on my back. I had a follow up appointment with my spine and pelvis doctor last week and he needs to clean up my L4 and L3 which are starting to grow together.

If they do not take care of it soon, the other vertebrae with eventually break down from working too hard. I am told it should only be about five days, although I have heard that before! As you could probably tell from the previous entries on my last twenty-day stay, I am ready to be done with surgery and hospitals. This will make five surgeries in ten months.

It has been a tough week as our family lost two friends, Dave Doyscher and Doug Swenson. Dave and Doug were both judges here in Minnesota and both from Forest Lake. Doug and Sandie were at the Forest Lake benefit in September that Dave and Gena Doyscher hosted for me. I still remember Doug's big smile that night.

I had a chance to visit with Dave just before Christmas at his home. I remember thinking as we talked that we were both a couple of beat-up old basketball players sharing stories of our glory days. One of my great experiences in life was when Dave invited me to sit on the bench with him in court. It was quite a shock when he turned to me at the end of a case and said, "What do you think we should do with this guy, Todd?"

I then realized how tough a job he had. I was grateful to know them.

So I go back to the hospital, big deal.

God bless you, and please include Gena Doyscher and family and Sandie Swenson and family in your prayers.

Todd

GUESTBOOK:

Todd,

Thank you so much for sharing your memories of David. It is comments like that that mean so much to our family. David thought the world of you and we were so happy that you came to visit.

When you have your next surgery, you can be assured prayers will be sent from the east shore of Clear Lake!

Blessings,

Gena Doyscher

———

Hi Todd,

Will send this for Dick as he doesn't use the computer, but he said he thinks of you all the time and was very happy that he had a chance to talk with you when you came to the Johnnie football game last fall. Dick said he talked to Jimmy Gagliardi about you and that he was going to check up on you, so hopefully he made contact.

After Dick visited with you, he was so impressed that you had remembered him by name. Dick is the ultimate Johnnie fan. We will keep you in our prayers and thoughts and hope all continues to go well for you.

Sincerely,

Dick and Theresa Doherty

LOOKING BACK...

It took me about a week after my last hospital visit to get back on my feet. After that, I made an appointment to visit Doctor Morgan to discuss the progress of my spine and pelvis over the course of these last months. That experience was shocking.

I had some X-rays done in Doctor Morgan's office. I spoke to a nurse and then an intern. These two gave me the impression that my back was healing nicely, so I was stoked to meet Doctor Morgan, shake his hand in victory, then leave his office sure of my back's healthy state of transition.

He took a look at my posture and said, "That's what I was worried about."

When the doctor came in he asked me to stand up for a minute. He took a look at my posture and said, "That's what I was worried about." He showed me my X-rays, and then he looked at me. I saw it in his eyes before he even uttered a word: I had to go back under the knife.

"We need to correct your back," Doctor Steve said. "If we don't, you're going to be in a really tough position."

I walked out of the doctor's office feeling like I'd been punched in the stomach—and my stomach doesn't do well with punches. I walked slowly through the cold, shuffling my feet. I got in my car, turned it on, and started crying. It just seemed like one thing after another.

Not only was I dealing with my own predicament, I was dealing with the deaths of some dear friends. How does this make any sense? These friends who have prayed for me and written to me, and all the while had their own issues they were dealing with. How is this fair?

These are people who are on my support team: they are supposed to be doing well too. I felt helpless. If I could have helped my friends conquer *this*—death—I would have done it. I would have helped them.

We were on the same team.

DAY 277

TUESDAY, MARCH 10, 2009

TODD: 11:13 AM

Hello everyone,

Sorry for the delay in getting back to you. It has been a while since I last wrote. I have had this desire to live a lot of life in these weeks before I go in again for surgery. The urgency of life is crystal clear.

It has been so much fun hanging out with my family. The kids are growing up so fast. I am so proud of how they've handled this disruption in family life. It is a lot of work for them and Erica and I am thankful for their fortitude. I hope that they are learning that, no matter what happens, you keep on fighting and keep on living.

We send our thoughts and prayers to Mike Grant and his extended family. Mike's mother, Pat, died this past week. Mike spoke at the Forest Lake benefit last fall and has been a close friend since my playing days back in the eighties.

We attended both Pat Grant's and Dave Doyscher's funerals these past few weeks. Both services were a celebration of life and it was so good to see so many friends.

My rehab is going well. I still have plenty of rehab exercises to do at home and only need to be at Courage Center once a week. It feels good to be making progress. I am still using my cane to walk and my stride is increasing.

My back surgery has been scheduled for April 2. It is about a four hour surgery and they plan on having me at Regions for five to seven days. They are telling me it will take three months to heal completely and then I can go bull riding and bungee jumping.

As I mentioned before, I am planning a "walking party" to thank you for all of your support. The party has been rescheduled twice now because of the two recent surgeries but I have secured a date that should work: Friday, June 5, from 6:00 to midnight at the Water Street Inn in Stillwater.

Please mark your calendars. There is no charge for this event—it is my family's way of saying thank you and celebrating our accomplishments together. I will send out additional updates as we get closer to the event. (Yes, June 5 is the date of the accident.)

Before I end, I wanted to share a recent little victory with you. A few weeks back Erica and I attended Dave Doyscher's funeral at Faith Lutheran in Forest Lake. I grew up in Forest Lake, my father was the pastor at Faith for twenty years, and our home was right behind the church.

There is no place on earth that feels as much like home to me as Faith Lutheran.

It is comforting to go back because so many of the people are the same. Pastor Phil worked with Dad in New Prague before we left for Forest Lake and then joined Dad again in Forest Lake a few years later. He is the one continuous connection to my childhood in New Prague and Forest Lake. It was comforting to hear Jim Lindstrom on the organ and to see the many familiar faces ushering and in the pews.

The usher came to seat us a few minutes before the service. Most everyone was seated, except for the family. The church was full and quiet as Jim played the organ. As the usher started to walk Erica and me to our seats, people saw me walking down the aisle with my cane. Suddenly they spoke up, saying, "Hey there's Todd," and "Way to go Todd."

It is an unusual experience, somewhat confusing and extremely humbling to be recognized that way in such a somber setting. It was like they had to speak but knew they were not supposed to. I felt awkward for a moment as I hoped it was not disrespecting Dave. As I sat down and saw his picture at the altar, I felt him smile at me. He and Gina organized the Forest Lake Benefit for me a few months earlier and I know it meant a lot to him for me to be there.

As I sat there during the service and took in all the familiar faces and surroundings, I could not help but think that this is what things would have looked like for me had I not survived the accident.

I thought of all the times I walked out of the sanctuary as an acolyte with my father, when I was confirmed, after Tim's funeral, as best man at Tami's wedding, and with Erica at my wedding.

So, my little victory . . . After they ushered out the Doyscher family our row was next. As I entered the center aisle next to Erica, I proudly tucked my cane along my side and—although it wasn't pretty—walked without assistance out of the church. Although much quieter this time, I heard the same words as I passed by those familiar faces: "Way to go, Todd."

I thank Dave for that opportunity and I will always remember that moment.

God bless you and your family,
Todd

GUESTBOOK:

Hi Todd,

It was good to read your update. You amaze me!

I have the same feelings about Forest Lake and Faith Lutheran. When we were at your benefit in the fall at Faith I felt so at home. It brought back a ton of memories, both good and bad: I thought about Tami's wedding as well as Tim's funeral and all the fun we had as kids growing up. I am glad I have those memories and I am glad I can still share them with you!

Love,

Kelly Beaudry

———

Oh Todd,

David would have been so happy to see you. I was so happy to see you and Erica and had heard of the "cheer" which is just great!

We owe our friendship with Mike Lovestrand to you, and it is yet another example of the interconnectedness we all have. We will be cheering for you on April 2 and successively as you recover fully. We hope to do a "walk about" on June 5. I note I am still using we, but I that is because David will still be with us in spirit!

Blessings to all of you,

Gena Doyscher

LOOKING BACK...

The funerals were hard to see. At both Pat's and Dave's funerals I received a glad response from mutual friends in such a somber setting. It was difficult to know how to react and maintain a sense of decorum.

Many people came up and just studied me. They hadn't seen me since before the accident. Some were surprised to see me on my feet; others were surprised to see me at all. The whole thing was very odd. It was especially surreal to experience these encounters at a close friend's funeral.

Many people came up and just studied me. They hadn't seen me since before the accident.

It's hard to lose friends, especially when I know it could have been me in their place. It doesn't seem right. I feel for them because I knew the struggles they had and the pain they'd been through. There is finality to their current condition, while my condition had an open-ended date.

My stuff is tiny compared to what they fought against with such dignity.

As I sat in the church and looked around, I thought to myself that this was pretty close to what it would look like at my funeral. These funerals plunged me into some very intense reflection. It all reminded me again just how very lucky I am.

DAY 284

TODD: 10:10 PM

Hello everyone,

Happy St. Patrick's Day!

I got the chance to go out and celebrate a little this afternoon at O'Gara's with Erica. We had a good time.

Things are good here as the kids have spring break and we have good weather. I'm enjoying watching them ride their bikes and explore the yard. It is so nice to get outside. The ice and snow limited my mobility and made every step a careful one, so I am happy to have the warm weather.

I have a couple of doctor's appointments this week and next to get ready for the April 2 surgery. Otherwise I am feeling pretty good. Things are slow for me but I am very grateful to be here.

I hope things are going well for you too.

God bless,

Todd

GUESTBOOK:

Howdy do,

I don't know the time right now . . . must just be Howdy Doody time, eh? I had a goofy dream and am up now for a few minutes for herbal tea. I checked for e-mails and found yours.

Oh, life . . . so many twists and turns, ups and downs, go-arounds. I like those the best—especially the slower times when I can enjoy the ride.

So Mary is seven years old . . . We are so blessed for the little ones in our lives bringing purpose and strength to the world in their own little ways. Such joy to see them age. Now my grandchildren and children see me age. Ouch.

I have been working/having fun as a volunteer with Art St. Croix, providing opportunities in the arts for adults with disabilities. You may have noticed some of our art and information on the walls at Courage Center. Your Mary's dear grandmother taught me a lot about the need for more services. This effort seems to be a link to her.

Time for tea.

Cheers and keep the faith,

Judy Gulden

LOOKING BACK...

I welcomed March because the ice was melting and I could walk outside, risk free. Just the feeling of spring in the air gave me momentum.

To celebrate St. Patrick's Day, Erica and I went to O'Gara's in St. Paul for a pint of Guinness, just as we had in previous years. Even though I still had the back surgery coming up, I felt pretty good. Whenever you're having something serious done, like surgery, you know it's a preemptive attack on what might go awry inside your body if you don't do it. I knew this, and so I was eager to take on whatever the surgeons had in store for me.

DAY 290

MONDAY, MARCH 23, 2009

TODD: 10:11 PM

Hello everyone!

I hope this finds you well. Spring is here and the flowers are not far behind. I can't wait for a few more days like last week!

We had a great weekend as we celebrated Mary's seventh birthday. It was very special to be here for it. I am so proud of her and the young lady she is.

Speaking of celebrating, today is my parents forty-sixth wedding anniversary! Way to go, Mom and Dad!

Rehab went very well today. I was able to accomplish a goal I had set about a month ago, another little victory. They had me practicing walking on a foam balance beam that's six inches wide and four feet long. It is tough to balance as I go heel, toe, heel, toe down the beam. When I get to the end they want me to go backwards to the start.

Each week I got closer but still needed assistance with the bars so I would not fall. Today, on my third try, I made it with no assistance. It felt great. I was very excited, as was Kelli, my physical therapist.

Setting big and little goals has been an important part of my recovery. I have set many goals during this process. When I did not make one I would set a new one. When I did make one I would make sure to enjoy the moment. I never focused on the failures, only on the successes.

Some goals were so small they seemed silly and others so big they seem impossible. But all of them—failures and successes alike—have helped me get to this point. I have a long, long way to go, but I have goals and will fight to accomplish each of them. I hope you are accomplishing your goals too!

God bless,

Todd

GUESTBOOK:

Todd,

Congrats for your accomplishment on the beam! Many of us cannot do it backwards, so you pat yourself on the back. May God continue to be with you and your family.

Marlene and Bill Burkhalter

LOOKING BACK...

When I was in the hospital it seemed like I was only piling up defeats. Now, out in the world again, I was collecting more and more victories. I was particularly focused on beating that foam balance beam at Courage Center.

> I could do whatever I set my mind to: I was proving this to myself daily.

Before the accident, I would have been able to walk this balance beam with my eyes closed, talking on the phone, and eating a hotdog at the same time. My injury, however, made this very challenging. After enough concentration and practice, I did it. I walked the beam.

I could do whatever I set my mind to: I was proving this to myself daily.

DAY 291

TUESDAY, MARCH 24, 2009

TODD: 9:49 PM

Today I wore flip flops for the first time in a long time. It was pretty cool and a nice change. My foot is starting to handle the weight better and is not as painful. The only problem was that one fell off and I did not realize it until Tim brought it back to me. I don't have much feeling in my right foot so it was hard to notice. They thought I looked a little silly.

> At least I have feeling in my legs—if my pants fell off and I didn't notice, well that would be a problem.

At least I have feeling in my legs—if my pants fell off and I didn't notice, well that would be a problem.

Goodnight and God bless!

Todd

GUESTBOOK:

Dear Todd,

Thanks for all the messages you leave on CaringBridge. They are always inspiring to us weaker mortals.

I know you are having surgery on Thursday. Please know that I and the Abbey community will remember you in prayer with the hope that it all goes easily, as swiftly as possible, and that the recovery is the same: swift and comfortable. Your journey from the accident to the present has been inspiring!

In Christ,

Don Talafous

LOOKING BACK...

It's funny to think I was pushing the envelope as I slid my toes into my spring flip flops. Wearing these shoes made my locomotion more difficult because I didn't have a lot of feeling in my feet and my toes don't bend much. I could put them on though, and I could get around all right. The point of wearing these was just that I wanted to fit in when that Minnesota summer rolled around. I didn't want the way I enjoyed life to change.

And that included wearing flip flops.

DAY 300

THURSDAY, APRIL 2, 2009

ERICA: 7:45 AM

Good morning everyone!

I am signing in from the one and only Regions Spa in St. Paul! Wow, I didn't miss this place. I am waiting to make some friends in the family waiting room since we will be here a while.

I just saw Todd off for his surgery. It is now 7:30 and they probably won't start the actual surgery for another hour. Dr. Morgan thinks it will take about six hours. He is having a spinal ostomy—I can't remember the full technical name now. It's early . . .

Basically in the accident, Todd's spine became detached from his pelvis. They fused the L5 to the S1 and pinned it. Well, as you know, Todd is superior at most things: evidently that includes bone growth. His bone is growing too much and fusing to the next two levels, and this is causing Todd to lean over. It happened because of his immobility after the accident.

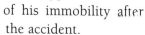

Basically in the accident, Todd's spine became detached from his pelvis.

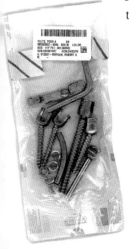

Dr. Morgan is going to take out some hardware and put some new hardware in. He is a great doctor, and he did the original surgery so he knows Todd's case very well.

That said, there's risk with any surgery, and especially with this one. I am asking you all to put your prayer hats back on for Todd today.

Heavenly Father, hold Todd in your hands today, extra tight. We love him and need him in our lives. Guide Dr. Morgan's hands to success. Help Todd heal quickly and give him strength to endure the pain.

Thank you all and I will keep you updated when I know something.

Love you all,

Erica

ERICA: 12:30 PM

Just a quick update. The nurse said that everything is going well, but it will be at least three more hours. Don't know much more, will keep you in the loop.

Thanks for those prayers,

Erica

ERICA: 4:20 PM

Good news, he just got out of surgery!

Have I ever mentioned that Todd was our miracle boy? Well, he is proving to be again. I talked to Dr. Morgan and he said that the surgery took a lot longer due to the massive bone that grew all the way up to the L3. Some of the ligaments had turned to bone as well, which is why the surgery took a lot longer than he anticipated. When he realized the amount of bone that grew, he saw that there wasn't a lot of protection from the nerves, so he had to take his time.

I asked about nerve damage and he said that he was getting all the signals he expected and more. The nerve that was severed in the L5 was getting a signal. He said that the L5 bone had fused and compressed so much that there wasn't any room for the nerve in there. But—here is the miracle part—he was getting a signal from that nerve. Yeah!

He was very happy with the correction he got in surgery and thinks Todd will be standing up straight in no time. Wow, the power of prayer!

I love you!

Erica

GUESTBOOK:

Hi Erica and Todd,

Praise the Lord, who evidently wants Todd around for awhile and who has such charisma. Will continue the prayers for continued recovery. Thanks for the recent update.

God bless!

Dick and Theresa Doherty

LOOKING BACK...

Though I was a little anxious going into surgery, I felt more secure about this back surgery than I did about the incisional hernia. Actually, I was more calm and collected than any of the other times I visited the hospital.

When Doctor Morgan came into the room to talk before I went under, I remember thinking that he seemed prepared for this operation too. I looked at him the way I would look at an athlete. He was in top form, ready to go.

I arrived around 6:00 in the morning, and the procedure took about eight hours. It was a long day and a short night.

DAY 303

SUNDAY, APRIL 5, 2009

ERICA: 4:21 PM

My goodness, I am so sorry that I have forgotten to update you all. Things have been very busy around here. Todd has done very well adjusting. He is in a significant amount of pain, but moving around. We're working on pain management.

The doctor signed off on his release today and he arrived back home around an hour ago. He's been sleeping ever since—that's the best thing for him now.

Thanks so much for all the well wishes and prayers. Indeed our Lord is good. We didn't expect him out for a least a week. I think he is trying to be a record breaker. Does that surprise anyone?

Love you all. Thank you for the notes, we love them.

Love,

Erica

GUESTBOOK:

Fultz Family,
Sunday night, and everyone there and accounted for at your home.
Beautiful.
Love, thoughts, prayers,
Judy Gulden

Way to go Todd, another victory—beating the hospital's prediction
of when you would come home after surgery! You continue to inspire
and amaze us all each and every day. We hope that you can get lots of
rest and regain your strength for your walking party! Here's to a speedy
recovery.
God bless you and your family,
Bridget and Joe Hammond

LOOKING BACK...

I woke up from the fog of surgery and the doctors had me up on my feet by the very next day. There was no pain: I couldn't have asked for a more steady operation, nor could I have asked for a more thorough doctor.

Doctor Morgan told me I had put in my time. He led me to the door, shook my hand, and after three days of recovery, he let me go.

That was the last time I was in Regions. My hope is that I don't make it back for a long time to come.

DAY 306

TODD: 10:41 PM

Hello everyone!

I'm back. I'm just a little slower, but getting better each day.

Thank you so much for your prayers and support this week. Once again my all-star support crew got me through! I am working hard on "good walking" and building up my strength for our party on June 5th. I can't wait to see you. I have some fun stuff planned.

> The pain is a pain, but hey, every day is beautiful. I sleep next to my wife each night and our three beautiful children run and jump on our bed each morning. Life is pretty darn good.

My hospital stay was short, which was great. My friend Amy, who was one of my first nurses (and one of the great ones), came to visit me. It was hard to believe it had almost been a year. She was excited to see me standing up, since she had me right after the accident when I was pretty messed up.

Dr. Morgan did a great job. I really enjoy him. He is the type of person who really cares about his patients. He is a good man.

I've been very tired since arriving home. The pain is a pain, but hey, every day is beautiful. I sleep next to my wife each night and our three beautiful children run and jump on our bed each morning. Life is pretty darn good.

God bless you!

Todd

GUESTBOOK:

Fultzer,

Great news to hear that you are doing good my friend. Just thinking of you pal, love your message about sleeping in your own bed. Sometimes it is the smallest things in life that can make a man so very happy.

Thoughts and prayers always,

Immer

Jeff Imsdahl

FOB Warrior/Kirkuk

LOOKING BACK...

My nurse, Amy, had pulled the dividing curtain around my bed and was administering a shot.

I heard John's voice call out. "Is Todd in here?" John is an old buddy of mine.

"Yes, he's behind the curtain," Amy responded.

"Yeah John, I'm just getting my sponge bath," I said, joking.

We had a good laugh, and then the curtain was pulled back. It was strange. We recognized each other's voices: that much was the same.

But when that curtain was pulled back and he saw me—his old buddy, Fultzy—lying there helpless, John started to cry. It was one of the most powerful moments I've ever experienced.

There are a lot of good memories I have collected in the aftermath of this accident. I've seen genuine and pure-hearted people rise to the occasion, meeting me when I needed their help. I hold these people very dear to my heart.

DAY 311

TODD: 9:33 PM

Hello everyone!

I hope you all had a great Easter. We sure enjoyed ours.

I was standing at the counter next to the toaster today when Madeline came up to me and said "Daddy, do you know how much I love you?"

"How much?" I asked.

She said "Google! It's the most."

I smiled and said thanks. Then she asked a question: "How much do you love me?"

I thought for a moment and said, "I love you so much that I am still here."

And she said, "How much is that Dad?"

I replied, "It pretty much blows Google out of the water!"

Life is worth fighting for. I thank you for all your support!

God bless,

Todd

GUESTBOOK:

Hey Todd and Erica,

Haven't written for a long time, but I am so encouraged with your progress. It will be five years on June 5 since my car accident and recovery is still happening. It's amazing what things are important to me today versus five years ago. Having the Lord as the center of my life and fully controlling what I do has brought me to a place of contentment that was never there before. I would let that accident happen all over again if it brought me to the same place I am today.

Don't you agree that you look at life entirely different than you did before? You want family and friends to understand how precious life is, but until they go through what we did, it's very hard for them to "get it."

Anyway, congrats on all the progress you have made. Ron and I really need to get together with the two of you sometime and reminisce a little bit. We love you guys and wish you all the best. The Lord bless you both. You are special and are being used for God's honor and glory.

Diane Hammes

LOOKING BACK...

I stood in the kitchen beside the toaster on the counter. Madeline walked over and the exchange she initiated with me was priceless. We learned something about each other that morning.

I wonder how my kids will look back on this year of accident and recovery. I know they see how others have interacted with their dad; I think that will stick with them. I just hope at the end of it all that they'll see that life is not necessarily fair, but if they keep their friends and family close, they'll have a support system around them. That way, they can accomplish anything.

DAY 328

TODD: 10:02 PM

Hello everyone!

Things are improving here. I am still walking with a cane but improving my stride.

My back is getting a little stronger each day. I still have pain but it is livable. I guess I just find ways to deal with it, since it seems to be a constant companion. I try and spend my time thinking about how lucky I am to be here rather than how tough it is sometimes.

I started back at work last week. I only work a few hours a day but it feels good to be back and contributing, although in a different way.

On my first day back I put on our new Hail Pros shirt and grabbed a new hat—thought I would look the part and feel like part of the team. But then I stopped and took off the hat. I thought about going back to work.

I went downstairs. In a back corner of boxes was one that had my name on it, followed by the word: Accident. I opened it. It contained items from my car that day, among them a beat-up Hail Pros hat. It too survived the accident.

> In a back corner of boxes was one that had my name on it, followed by the word: Accident.

As I put it on I paused for a moment. It was quiet in the basement. I was overcome with pride: another step back to life, another step closer, and another little victory.

I have worn that hat each day since.

GUESTBOOK:

Todd,

It is so great to be reminded of the little things in life that are important. We take it for granted and it's nice to be brought back to what is truly significant.

Your stories have so much inspiration, I really enjoy them. Now that spring is around and we are out more we realize how much we miss you in our neighborhood and the daily little chats we'd have with you guys.

So strange that it is almost a year since your accident. I remember the day so well. The progress you have made is amazing, and we continue to pray and think of you. Take care, we'll see you June 5th. Keep in touch!

Much love,

Andrea and Jim Sprenger

———

Hi Todd,

Even though I check your updates frequently I never take the time to send a message of encouragement. Today on my way to work, traffic was backed up because of an accident. On my way home it was once again backed up due to an accident.

The one tonight was not a pretty sight . . . the cars looked similar to yours. I thought of you when I saw the cars and thought how wonderful it is that you were able to make it through it. It is great to read about your improvements and what a great attitude you have towards improving and life in general. I think of you often and hope that we can make it to the party on the 5th with the Duponts.

Roxane Tolle

LOOKING BACK...

I was glad to go back to work and contribute. At that point, my office was in an addition we'd built onto the house. Getting there meant walking about ten steps through my walk-in closet. They humored me, giving me things to do. I worked a few hours here, a few hours there. It wasn't anything like full speed, but even so, it was good to be back.

DAY 353

TODD: 11:47 PM

Hi everyone!

Hope you are well.

Great news . . . I kicked the bottom of my desk today with my foot and it hurt like heck!

Erica was wondering why I was laughing and in such pain at the same time—I think she thought I was losing it.

I have had so little feeling in my foot I didn't expect to feel it when it happened. I was happy to be in pain again! I don't have total feeling in the foot but it is coming back in spots.

Who knows, I might kick something tomorrow too!

Please make sure you let our mutual friends know about the party.

God Bless!

Todd

GUESTBOOK:

Fultz family,

Marshall, Howard, and I went up north camping for the long weekend. While we were there we met a gentleman named David. Howard, being very shy, shocked me when he would walk up to David and sit on his lap around the campfire. He talked to him and pointed out everything under the sun, just as if he had known this stranger his whole life.

The pain of seeing this actually brought me joy because somehow, on this particular weekend, I saw my dad. He came in a different form and in a man that loved to fish (Dad was not a fisherman). This stranger brought me joy and sadness in the same moment. I completely understand! May your joy and your pain be a sign that God continues to use you even when things are not always as they should be. And may he give you peace in a time of trial, even if it is just for a moment!

All our love,

Karen Nelson

LOOKING BACK...

The body can take a long time to heal. I still experienced numbness in my forearms, my thighs, and my feet, but I also occasionally felt tingles and sensations.

After feeling it for a long time, pain becomes a constant companion. You try to learn to live with that pain, to divert it, or to occupy your mind with something else. It doesn't go away. My right ankle is *always* in pain. I will probably always have that, but it's a constant reminder of what I've overcome and what I'm capable of.

DAY 360

MONDAY, JUNE 1, 2009

TODD: 11:19 PM

Hello everyone,

Great news! Kelli, my physical therapist at the Courage Center, has moved me to once a month instead of once a week. She is very pleased with my recovery and feels my progress will continue to improve. I still use the cane, but I'm always getting closer to walking without assistance.

I am very excited to see everyone on Friday. Erica and I have been looking forward to this day for a long time.

Remember that kids are welcome. We have some fun stuff planned. It will be great to look you in the eye this time! I put a new picture up from Scott Ledoux's benefit a few weeks ago. Scott is a friend of mine and I ask that you say a prayer for him as he battles ALS. He has an incredible spirit and it was so good to see him.

One of the toughest aspects of my own recovery has been watching friends dealing with life's challenges when they're not getting the same daily improvements in their recovery that I've enjoyed in mine. It is tough to deal with—humbling and confusing to say the least.

Your prayers have comforted me and my family during these challenges. I have had a number of prayer requests during this time. Thank you for the many times you have included my friends in your prayers.

I appreciate it.

God bless you! And I am hugging every one of you on Friday.
Todd

GUESTBOOK:

Todd,

Hurray-a Tuesday . . . and the sun is shining. Rain or shine, it is a new day. I happen to be home from work today, so am lovin' this time.

It is always good to read your entries. Did I read the numbers right? How many hits have you had on your site?

It's great to have Courage Center so close. It is a place of positive energy and kindness to all. Glad you are down to once a month. Check out the art. Some of Art St. Croix's artworks are still on display.

See you Friday.

Judy Gulden

LOOKING BACK...

The walking party at the Water Street Inn was great. About 300 people showed up, so I saw all the faces that had written so many kinds words over the course of the year. I was able to get up on stage, introduce my family, and spend a few minutes thanking everyone.

I have vivid memories of all the kids running around and playing video games. We passed out prizes, we ate, and we relaxed. It was a powerful night for me, the night of June 5th.

I had come full circle. I remembered all of the events that had passed over those twelve months, and to see this glorious celebration at the completion of the circle was so empowering.

I stayed up very late that night. I remember looking down at my watch as the minute hand ticked into the next day. June 5th came and went. I took a moment to digest the reality of that transition. I had a feeling, but what was it exactly? Closure.

DAY 373

SUNDAY, JUNE 14, 2009

TODD: 11:37 PM

Hello everyone,

Hope you all had a great weekend.

I had a follow up appointment with my spine doctor this past week and everything is looking good. I have two more scheduled in the next few weeks for my spine and legs. Hopefully these will go as well and we can move on with life.

I will keep the CaringBridge site open until my next two appointments as they are kind of the last hurdle in determining if any additional surgeries are needed.

It was so good to see everyone last week. I had the most wonderful time.

There are very few moments in life that will match the love, gratitude, and energy in that room. I will remember that night for the rest of my life.

Thanks again and God bless!

Todd

GUESTBOOK:

Thank you for a great time! Howard (grandson) thought it was the best party ever and named the bear he won "Todd Bear."

It was great to see you up and at 'em!

Gena Doyscher

———

What a fantastic evening to celebrate Todd's incredible recovery and the wonderful family who has loved and supported him through all of this! The Fultz family is truly an inspiration and we are better people for knowing all of you. How fun it was to see so many people who love and admire you guys.

God bless,

The Karlstads

LOOKING BACK...

The walking party at the Water Street Inn was great. About 300 people showed up, so I saw all the faces that had written so many kinds words over the course of the year. I was able to get up on stage, introduce my family, and spend a few minutes thanking everyone.

I have vivid memories of all the kids running around and playing video games. We passed out prizes, we ate, and we relaxed. It was a powerful night for me, the night of June 5th.

I had come full circle. I remembered all of the events that had passed over those twelve months, and to see this glorious celebration at the completion of the circle was so empowering.

All right, that's over, I thought. Now let's go live.

I stayed up very late that night. I remember looking down at my watch as the minute hand ticked into the next day. June 5th came and went. I took a moment to digest the reality of that transition. I had a feeling, but what was it exactly? Closure.

All right, that's over, I thought.

Now let's go live.

EPILOGUE

ONE JOURNEY AMONG MANY

This journey I embarked on after the accident is one of many I will have in my life. In our lives we will experience great change and some epic challenges.

This journey pushed my limits both mentally and physically, but through it all I have found the fortitude and passion to conquer these challenges and the resiliency to accommodate the changes.

My life is not much different than yours! All of us will face adversity throughout our lifetimes, but deep within each of us is the ability to overcome. Each of us has a tremendous life in front of us.

This experience has taught me the value of persistence, the deep love of friends and family, and the urgency in life. Through it all I have developed an overwhelming gratefulness for each day.

In the end this is a book about all of us, about what we can overcome together. Carry on a good fight, focus on the positives in life, and celebrate each victory along the way!

CARINGBRIDGE GUESTBOOK ENTRIES

FRIDAY, JUNE 6, 2008 8:42 PM, CDT

You are in my thoughts. I know it will be tough, but I am confident that you have the motivation and strength for a most speedy recovery!
Jessica Buege

SATURDAY, JUNE 7, 2008 7:32 PM, CDT

Todd and Erica,
You are all in my thoughts in prayers during this hard time. I know that the Lord is and has been with you the past few days. Please let me know if you need anything: cleaning, helping with the kids, transportation, etc. Please use me anyway you can.
Marita Metcalf

SATURDAY, JUNE 7, 2008 9:27 PM, CDT

Dear Erica, Mary, Timothy and Madeline,
May the Lord bless you and keep you in His grace.
I thank and praise the Lord that Todd is safe and in His care. I know this is true. God will not forget Todd (Isaiah 49:15-17). God has engraved Todd's name upon the palm of his hand!
May the Lord guide and watch over the care and healing given by Todd's doctors and nurses.
I will keep you all in my prayers for the many weeks of recovery. Peace be with you always.
Love,
Uncle Phil

SATURDAY, JUNE 7, 2008 10:18 PM, CDT

Hi Erica and Todd and family,

Erica, what can I say? I was shocked when church phoned me yesterday with the news about Todd. I just want you to know that we are so thankful Todd made it through such a horrible accident, and that we are continually praying for you and thinking of you.

If there is anything I can do, please let me know. I would love to have the kids or whatever is needed. My heart goes out to you and your family. May God's blessings and healings pour over your family at this time.

Love you and God bless,

Kim Jelinek

SUNDAY, JUNE 8, 2008 8:23 AM, CDT

Fultz family,

The Simcik clan is praying for you (x6). The boys could not believe the pictures of the car. I am sure we said a prayer for Todd right after the accident, since we pray for injured people each time we hear Life Link fly near us! Sounds like it will be a long road to recovery, so please lean on friends and church to help out. In Him,

Deb and Matt Simcik and boys

SUNDAY, JUNE 8, 2008 10:00 AM, CDT

Dear Fultz family,

My prayers and thoughts are with you all. I know Todd has faced lots of trials in his life and will overcome this also. I also know he is in the best hospital for trauma and I will pray for the doctors and nurses caring for him. God bless you all.

Jan Ramboldt

Dear Todd and family,

Life really throws some curveballs, but so glad to hear you are on the road to catch it and throw it back. You are in our prayers. The future will be a challenge but God will provide for your needs.

We are so glad you have set up this page to keep us informed. We will check it often. You have lots of family and friends to lean on for support.

Love you all,

Laurie and Steve Iverson

I just heard about the accident and cannot imagine what you are going through. Please make sure you ask for help—you are going to need it in the coming months. We are praying for a recovery that is as fast and pain free as possible. He is one lucky guy: Regions is great, they will take good care of him.

Take care, our thoughts are with you!

Jen Selleck (Luebben)

Fultzie,

You are in our thoughts and prayers. Godspeed on your recovery.

Varls and Steph (Steve Varley)

P.S. "I'm in, I'm in, I'm in."

Todd and Erica and family,

You are in our thoughts and prayers as you go through these difficult times. God's blessings to you.

Lee and Sandi Poppe

SUNDAY, JUNE 8, 2008 3:28 PM, CDT

Todd,

So sorry to hear about the accident. Take it one day at a time and with God's gracious love and guidance you'll get through this. Our prayers and thoughts are with you. Your Aunt Edna sends her prayers too!

Joan and Jack Iverson

SUNDAY, JUNE 8, 2008 7:18 PM, CDT

Todd and family,

Know that you are in my thoughts and prayers. Here's wishing each of you peace and to Todd a speedy and full recovery.

Kevin Johnson

MONDAY, JUNE 9, 2008 7:34 AM, CDT

Dear Todd and family,

Deer hunting helped us to know a person who is giving and loving, full of spirit and energy, always with a smile on his face and something good to say.

Getting this e-mail was a shock to us and we hope (and know) that you will fully recover. If there is anything we can do or help with, please let us know. May God be with you on your way of recovery. May he be with your family to be strong and able to see the sometimes little and other times bigger steps toward full recovery.

The Zieglers, Martin, Joyce, and Girls

MONDAY, JUNE 9, 2008 8:20 AM, CDT

Dear Fultz family,

We're thinking about you guys and will continue to during your recovery.

Love,

Dono, M, Preston, and Kendal Grant

Todd and the Fultz family,

All of you are in our prayers. We pray for the wisdom and knowledge of your caregivers at this time. The body is amazing with the power to heal with time and care. May you find comfort knowing the Lord is with you and also comes to you through the people around you. May you feel the peace and strength of God as your healing journey continues.

Carole England, A Tanzania Traveler

Todd, Erica, and family,

I've thought of you and your family often this weekend after I heard of the accident. Prayers are being sent your way for a speedy and full recovery. Give all of your kids a big hug from Ms. Shannon. Tim is so good about giving out those hugs—tell him it's my turn. I look forward to hearing about your recovery.

God's Peace, Shannon Goldstein

Todd/Erica et al,

I'm so sorry. Our prayers are with you all! Take it one day at a time and may you experience God's peace each moment, each day. We will keep you in our thoughts and prayers! Remember, one day at a time.

Kari and Hoien boys

Ellen and I are so glad to hear that things are improving. We wish you a speedy recovery. Thank goodness we have so many great medical people to help us in times like these. You are all in our thoughts and prayers every day! God bless,

Rodney and Ellen Erickson

Todd, Erica and family,

We just heard about Todd's awful accident and are so sorry that you are having to deal with all of the pain and recovery. Please know that you are in our prayers and we would love to help in any way possible!

Brent, Jess, Char, and Blaine Batchelor

Hi Eunice and Don, Erica, Todd, and family,

I am a pastor at Christ the King Lutheran Church and was in Africa recently with Don and Eunice. I also saw you at Synod Assembly. I am so sorry to hear of Todd's accident and so grateful to read of his slow, but positive, steps toward recovery.

Having been there with our son-in-law who was in the I-35 bridge collapse, our family knows well about those anxious days and nights at the hospital and the power of prayer and support through CaringBridge. The Birkeland family sends their love and prayers and we know that God is good, all the time, and that Christ will surround and uphold you through this time.

Blessings and peace,

Pastor Deborah Birkeland

To the entire Fultz family,

We want you to know that you all are in our thoughts and prayers. Writing something here is tough because words don't say how deeply we feel. We stand ready to help in any way we can. We are praying for you Todd!

Dave and Lori Purdy, Chad Olson, and Alison Vruno

Please know there are many, many people out here watching, reading, praying, and pulling for Todd. We know it's going to be long and hard. These are the worst days so we send you all our positive thoughts and energy to sustain and lift you up.

God bless Todd and all his family and friends,
Diane Borle

Todd, Erica and kids,
I wish you the best of luck and you are in our prayers.
Amy (Sonju) Tuttle

Fultz family,
Our thoughts and prayers are with your whole family. May God bless you all and hold you tight in his hands.
Scott, Lena, and Gracie Ann Erickson

Lavon and I profoundly empathize with you/yours at this time of trauma and hope. May the Healer touch you.
Lyle Lutz

Hang in there Todd! We're all pulling for you in Tracy!
Thinking of you,
The Kainz and Fultz family

Dear Todd, Erica, and family,

We were so sad to hear about Todd's accident, but also so thankful that he survived. We know he will pull through. You guys are both so strong and have so many people around you who love and support you.

Please know you are in our thoughts for a speedy and full recovery, Todd. Erica, keep your chin up—one day at a time.

Erich and Yunny send their best to you as well.

Thinking of all of you,

Alexis and Jamie Moore

Fultz family,

We were so saddened to hear the news of Todd's accident, but so very thankful to hear that he will be OK. Please know your entire family is in our thoughts and prayers. If you need help with anything over the next few months, we are here. The kids are welcome anytime, we are just down the road.

Take care and God bless,

Jen and Chris Cosgrove

Todd and family,

Wishing you a speedy recovery. We will keep you in our thoughts and prayers.

Mike Ramler

MONDAY, JUNE 9, 2008 2:25 PM, CDT

Fultz family,

We heard about the accident. Our thoughts are with you all right now. The girls would love to have the kids at our house to play so if you ever need that or anything else don't hesitate! We will continue to send all good thoughts your way!

Chris, Michelle, Claire, and Sophie Bressler

MONDAY, JUNE 9, 2008 3:33 PM, CDT

Todd,

I know you are a fighter and will come out on top with a story to tell. We are praying for your healing and fast recovery. Erica, we are praying for peace in your heart that all will be fine. God performs amazing miracles. Serese and Brian Honebrink

MONDAY, JUNE 9, 2008 3:34 PM, CDT

We just received an e-mail which told about Todd's accident. We are saddened about the news. Our hearts go out to you.

We have come to know Todd through his parents and by reading the book Tiger Tim which describes the special relationship of love and care he had for his brother.

We recall the story about the promise he made to Tim to point one finger heavenward as a signal to his brother that he is grateful for Tim's leadership in living and fighting battles. He learned from Tim a "never-give-up attitude."

From the reflections in the daily journal about Todd, there is bountiful evidence that the God-given never-give-up attitude abides and sustains him now.

We will join with many others in offering prayers for healing, strength, and patience for Todd and his family.

Love, Jerry and Joan Hoffman

MONDAY, JUNE 9, 2008 4:24 PM, CDT

Hello Fultz family,

We were so saddened to hear the news. Todd, we have you and your family in our prayers. Also, we have added your name to two church prayer lists. With the power of prayer, support from your family and friends, and your own inner strength, we know this difficult time will be overcome! Please give Madeline and Timmy a hug from us. Please do not hesitate to call or e-mail us if we can help in any way.

Maria Sanocki and Amy Ayers, LADC teachers

MONDAY, JUNE 9, 2008 4:31 PM, CDT

Todd and Erica,

Our thoughts and prayers are with you in the days ahead.

Jen Hines and the 3M Championship Crew

MONDAY, JUNE 9, 2008 7:35 PM, CDT

Todd, Erica, and family,

My thoughts and prayers are with you at this time. Todd, I know you will make a speedy recovery. Please let us know if there is anything we can do for you. Take care.

Leslie Stockey, 3M Championship

MONDAY, JUNE 9, 2008 7:40 PM, CDT

Todd,

You da man, and always will be. A great competitor and person and a better friend. There are many more fish to be caught. Thoughts and prayers are with you all.

Mike, Colleen, Ryan, Taylor (The Grants)

MONDAY, JUNE 9, 2008 9:24 PM, CDT

Fultz family,

We are so sorry to hear about the terrible accident. You are all in our thoughts and prayers. Please know we are here for you . . .

Danielle and David Gackstetter

MONDAY, JUNE 9, 2008 9:24 PM, CDT

Todd,

My thoughts and prayers are with you and your family. I know you are a fighter!

My best,

Charlie Divitto

TUESDAY, JUNE 10, 2008 5:29 AM, CDT

Todd, Erica, and family,

We were all so sorry to hear about the accident. Our thoughts and prayers are with you all. Our hope now is to see you all in Ireland as soon as possible.

Mary, Rory, Kathy, Liz, and Jim Seeley

TUESDAY, JUNE 10, 2008 8:34 AM, CDT

Fultz family,

You are in the thoughts and prayers of many of the people of this country and certainly as news reaches Africa the prayers will be coming from around the world. Praying for strength for all of you and the doctors for the knowledge they will need to give the treatment Todd will need for healing and recovery. May you feel God's presence each day.

Jan Stevens

TUESDAY, JUNE 10, 2008 8:37 AM, CDT

Erica and family,

We are so sorry to hear about Todd. Our thoughts and prayers are with you. Please let us know if there is anything we can do for you. God bless.

Jason and Marti Trent

TUESDAY, JUNE 10, 2008 8:40 AM, CDT

Todd, Erica, and kids,

We are so sorry to hear about the accident. You are a strong family with tons of strength and support. You are all in our thoughts.

Gretchen, Brian, Isaac, AJ, and Sam Gunderson

TUESDAY, JUNE 10, 2008 9:38 AM, CDT

Todd and family,

You are in our thoughts and prayers today and will remain there until Todd is home.

Steve Schmitz and family

TUESDAY, JUNE 10, 2008 9:39 AM, CDT

Todd, Erica, and family,

We want you to know that you are in our thoughts and prayers.

Tara, Tom, Claire, Maggie, and Laci Wagner

TUESDAY, JUNE 10, 2008 10:57 AM, CDT

Dear Erica, Todd, and family,

This morning I received an e-mail about your accident. From the moment I read it I had goosebumps. I enjoyed spending time with you at Bridget and Joe's wedding. Please know that I am thinking about you! You are in my thoughts and prayers.

Laurie Wright (Stillwater High School–San Francisco, CA)

TUESDAY, JUNE 10, 2008 11:34 AM, CDT

Fultz family,

The Klassen crew is busy praying! We are thinking of you every minute and are available for anything you need any minute of the day. You both have the spirit and the determination to get through any obstacle in your way.

Melanie Klassen

TUESDAY, JUNE 10, 2008 12:45 PM, CDT

Todd, Erica and family,

You will be in our prayers every day and we look forward to a Central-7 get together this fall with the whole gang. Hope to see your smiling face soon. . .

Mike Sullivan and family

TUESDAY, JUNE 10, 2008 2:02 PM, CDT

Hopefully all goes well and we see you in Ireland again with Todd fine and well!

Philip Seeley and family

TUESDAY, JUNE 10, 2008 2:28 PM, CDT

Todd and family,

Our thoughts and prayers are with you.

Brad, Mary, Pat, Owen, Luke, Will, and Ava Blascziek

TUESDAY, JUNE 10, 2008 2:35 PM, CDT

Todd and family,

Our prayers are with you in these trying times. We know God is holding you close and giving all of you strength for the coming days.

Love,

Bill and Jeri Kuecks

TUESDAY, JUNE 10, 2008 2:50 PM, CDT

Todd and family,

Thoughts and prayers are with you and the family. The Fultzy I know is a fighter and champion, and will have a speedy recovery. Good luck tomorrow. I will be thinking of you.

God bless!

Mike and Katie Magnuson

TUESDAY, JUNE 10, 2008 2:52 PM, CDT

Todd and family,

I know we've met once. Gunnar and Thor went to preschool with Tim. We are so sorry to hear of your tragedy. If there is anything that we can do for you, please let us know. We are keeping you in our thoughts and prayers.

Sincerely,

The Johnsons, Paul, Sharri, Gunnar, Thor, and Elsa

TUESDAY, JUNE 10, 2008 3:21 PM, CDT

Fultz family,

I don't know you, but know friends of yours: sort of a one-degree-of-separation. We just went through a huge medical crisis ourselves and just wanted you to know that we're praying for you and your family. These are hard times, but it is so great and so important that you have so many friends and family around to be supportive. Get well!

Love and prayers, Adam Swenson

Todd, Erica, Don, Eunice, and Kids

*Just found the link. Please, all of you hang in there and know you
are surrounded by healing angels and caring hands and hearts. You are
in our prayers. On a personal note, Todd (hunting buddy) get strong, get
well. The members of the "New Prague Ballet and Rifle Team" are there
for you and will do whatever is needed to help. Erica, we can babysit or
whatever you need. Just call . . .*

Tim and Deb Miller

Best of luck tomorrow. Dave and I are thinking of you guys.
Greg and Dave, Wildlife Specialties, Inc.

Todd and family,

*My prayers are with you all. I have no doubt that God will see you
through this tough time. From my experience, Todd has all of the strength
and courage to conquer any obstacle. This will be no different! God bless.*

Adam Landeen

Todd, Erica, and family:

*Such a shock to hear about Todd's accident. Life is so fragile. At
times it is hard to understand what life dishes out. But one thing you can
count on are friends and family who deeply care and pray that each new
day will be better than the last. Our prayers are with you, get well soon.*

Bob and Kathy Warn

TUESDAY, JUNE 10, 2008 6:31 PM, CDT

Erica and family,

I was just shocked to hear of Todd's accident. Life's challenges are unbelievable at times, but know the love and support you have out there for Todd. My prayers are with you all and I know God's strength is with him. If I can assist with the kids or whatever, please let me know.

In Him, Rachelle and John Quinn

TUESDAY, JUNE 10, 2008 6:58 PM, CDT

Fultz, Erica, and kids,

Boyle let us know of your CaringBridge site. My first reaction was, whew, you don't get a CaringBridge site for being dead. By the looks of the pictures you had a divine copilot to get you through, and he is still there.

You are a strong fighter and, as of this moment, have 1,567 visitors thinking of you and praying for you and your family.

We pray for your full and speedy recovery. In Jesus name, our Creator, Lord and Savior, Amen.

Dan, Connie, Mitchell, and Megan Mattison

TUESDAY, JUNE 10, 2008 7:51 PM, CDT

Fultz family,

You are in our thoughts and prayers as you begin your recovery. Good luck in the weeks and months ahead.

Jed, Jenny, Emma, and T.J. Cass

TUESDAY, JUNE 10, 2008 7:56 PM, CDT

Todd and family,

We've been praying for you since we heard about the accident. Stay strong and we'll pray for the surgery to go well tomorrow.

The Parringtons

TUESDAY, JUNE 10, 2008 8:16 PM, CDT

To the Fultz family,

We have just learned of the accident and will, of course, keep all of you in our prayers. I am an old friend of Todd dating back to third or fourth grade. Through the years, we have periodically run into each other and each other's friends and always have good things and stories to tell. We wish you the best and will be checking on Todd's progress.

Mike Buckingham

TUESDAY, JUNE 10, 2008 9:20 PM, CDT

Fultz family,

Heard about Todd's accident over the weekend. Our thoughts and prayers will be with you as you head to surgery tomorrow and in the weeks to come as you recover.

Donnie and Lisa (Solheid) Simon

TUESDAY, JUNE 10, 2008 9:38 PM, CDT

Erica, Todd, and kids,

Just heard the news today about the accident. So sorry to hear about Todd's injuries, but after reading your journal its sounds like he's slowly on the road to recovery. Thinking of your family during this time.

Tell Mary that Tessa (from preschool) says hello and she hopes her dad gets better.

Kim and Pete Venuta

TUESDAY, JUNE 10, 2008 9:52 PM, CDT

Todd and Erica,

We just wanted to let you know we are thinking of you all and praying that Todd has a speedy and successful recovery. Even though we are in Forest Lake please let us know if there is anything we can do for you or the kids. Regards, Ryan and Carrie Dillon

TUESDAY, JUNE 10, 2008 9:55 PM, CDT

Fun Todd, Erica and Kids,

We have been thinking about you guys a ton. While you work on healing, know that we are all praying for you. These are definitely tough times, but with Todd's determination, spirit, and the support of friends and family we know he will get through it. We will be thinking about and praying for you during surgery tomorrow!

Love, Jim and Sara McGrath

TUESDAY, JUNE 10, 2008 10:01 PM, CDT

Todd and family,

Our hearts and prayers go out to you as you fight your way back. Your guestbook reflects the feelings of so many people whose lives you have touched and who care for you and will be there in the days to come.

Sandy and Jerry Robinson

WEDNESDAY, JUNE 11, 2008 7:07 PM, CDT

Todd, Erica and family,

We are thinking about you all the time and are so thankful that today's surgery is going well. Todd is such a fighter and with the all prayers that are with you today from so many family and friends, we are so very hopeful that he can begin to turn the corner. His positive attitude and optimistic spirit are contagious and we know they're helping him get through today. Blessings to your family. Ted and Kathy Saltzman

WEDNESDAY, JUNE 11, 2008 8:04 AM, CDT

Fultz family,

I'm sitting in my condo in downtown St. Paul right now looking at Regions and thinking and praying hard for Todd and his ten-hour surgery. What a wonderful, energetic, strong person Todd is. I just know he will get through this. Hilary (nee Doyscher) and Mark Cheeley

Erica and Todd,

We are praying for you all day and every day!

Dan and Jen Sletten and the boys

My thoughts are with you and your family. I will light a candle and make sure we support you in our prayers.

Shawn Crist

May your hearts continue to be touched and warmed by the generous outpouring of God's love and support that is being expressed through so many for you, Todd, and your family. My thoughts and prayers are with you that the surgery will be successful.

My best to you on your journey of recovery,

Carol Boyle

We are thinking and praying for you today! May God guide the hands of those helping Todd today and may His peace and blessings surround and embrace all of you.

The Lysne family

Todd,

We hope and pray for you to gain a full recovery from this tragedy. May you find peace and courage to get through this difficult time. We know you are a champion and will fight each day to get back your strength and health!

Sincerely, Janel and Dean Wahlin

WEDNESDAY, JUNE 11, 2008 12:33 PM, CDT

Dear Todd and family,

Understandably, we've fallen out of touch as people do when they leave high school. The pictures on this site really brought everything back home for me, because I also have a family and I can still, in my vaguest of recollections, remember laughing with you and enjoying your company. It's hard for me to imagine what you and your family are going through. I will keep you in my prayers. Best wishes and God bless. If there is any way I can contribute, please give me a call.

Patrick Cameron

WEDNESDAY, JUNE 11, 2008 12:47 PM, CDT

Fultzy,

Saddened to learn about your accident, but anyone tough enough to track and film Bobcat Brown in the wild can make it through this! Get well soon; maybe there's a twenty-year anniversary revisit of Johnnie Sports Tonight in our future! Our thoughts and prayers are with you.

John and Mary Tuvey and family

WEDNESDAY, JUNE 11, 2008 1:16 PM, CDT

Todd, Erica, and family,

We were shocked and saddened to hear of the accident. We are following your progress and our thoughts and prayers are with you and your family. Your spirit and attitude will only serve to hasten your recovery, and we all look forward to the day you go home.

Dan and Carla Hale

WEDNESDAY, JUNE 11, 2008 2:00 PM, CDT

Todd, Erica, and family,

We were sad to hear about the accident. You and your family are in our thoughts and prayers during surgery and the road to recovery. Get well soon.

Shantell, Mike, Merina, Storm, and Radian Lenz

WEDNESDAY, JUNE 11, 2008 2:05 PM, CDT

Todd and family,

Toni told us about your horrible accident. Just know our thoughts and prayers are with you and your family. We wish you a speedy recovery.

Mike and Judy Erickson

WEDNESDAY, JUNE 11, 2008 2:13 PM, CDT

Hi Todd and family, we were very sad to learn of your accident. Our thoughts and prayers are with you all as Todd recovers and heals from this horrible ordeal.

Take care,

Darren, Terra, Lindsey, and Hailey Johnson

WEDNESDAY, JUNE 11, 2008 2:32 PM, CDT

Todd, Erica, and family,

My heart goes out to all of you. You have always had so many fans, and right now we are all rallying around you praying for your recovery!

Teresa (Nickila) Ebertz

WEDNESDAY, JUNE 11, 2008 4:35 PM, CDT

Fultzy,

Godspeed in your recovery. All you single digit guys seem to have a way to bounce back quickly! Get well man!

Tom Riitters

WEDNESDAY, JUNE 11, 2008 4:43 PM, CDT

Todd and Erica,

You are in our thoughts and prayers. May your bright smiles and faith see you through the days ahead.

Love, Lisa, Nick, and Chris Imsdahl

WEDNESDAY, JUNE 11, 2008 5:33 PM, CDT

My family will pray for you and your family from Seattle tonight. Heal up Fultzy!

Tom George

WEDNESDAY, JUNE 11, 2008 6:32 PM, CDT

Dear Fultz family,

We are so happy to hear the surgery is going well. You have been in our prayers. Erica, please know I am available to watch the kids, etc. May God continue to heal Todd!

Love, Laura and David Tussey

WEDNESDAY, JUNE 11, 2008 7:32 PM, CDT

Todd and Erica and children; Don and Eunice and Tami,

We have followed this site and continued to pray for Todd and all of you throughout the day. So glad to hear that all is going well so far. I know that God is holding him and all of you in His protecting arms. We will continue to be in touch.

With love, Alice Holm

WEDNESDAY, JUNE 11, 2008 8:16 PM, CDT

Fultzy and family, We are keeping you and your family in our thoughts and prayers. We know you are giving this everything you got (as always) and we are all supporting you. That fighting spirit that is admired by all. Godspeed, Fultzy!

Flynner

Fultzy, We just heard the news and you and your family are in our prayers. We wish you the best and a very speedy recovery.

Matt and Christine (Letsche) Winston

Hi, Glad Todd is moving toward healing with this surgery behind him. All of you are held in God's love and my prayers along with the prayers of God's people at Trinity.

Peace and prayers, Kris Linner

Todd and family,

We are so glad to hear your surgery went well. You are in our thoughts and prayers. Get well soon.

Jon, Kay, Zach and Mitch Gerlach

Todd and family,

I want you to know that you are in my thoughts and prayers during this very difficult time. As I read the guestbook I can see how you have touched many lives, as I'm sure you are doing at the hospital and yet to come. I will continue to pray for strength for you and your family and wisdom for doctors taking care of you!

Take care, Cindy (Lakso) Lane

Todd, Erica, and family,

I was on the CaringBridge website for my sister-in-law who had a brain aneurysm last Thursday and decided to visit your site. Your dad was our pastor for many years and members of our church have been praying hard for you since your accident. God's angels have been hard at work with

you and with my sister-in-law, Karen. We do have an awesome God. We
shall continue to pray that you will be blessed daily with healing and hope.

Jeanette and Richard Hahn

WEDNESDAY, JUNE 11, 2008 11:14 PM, CDT

Todd and family,

Being almost 1,000 miles away from the Twin Cities, news of acci-
dents in the SJU football family take a little while to get out to Montana.
I was reviewing D3 football tonight and caught the news of your accident.
You and your family are in the thoughts and prayers of my family. I was
glad to hear of the success with today's surgeries. You were truly one of
the great SJU football leaders and always an inspiration.

I will never forget the tribute to your brother after every touchdown.

Jeff Bretherton

THURSDAY, JUNE 12, 2008 7:24 AM, CDT

Erica,

Allison informed me of this accident and website. I wish you and
your family continued strength through all of this. In these types of situ-
ations time is so important to the healing process, so be patient and take
baby steps. Incremental improvements beat postponed perfection!

It is evident you and Todd have an extensive network of friends and
family and we all will be sending our continued love and support. Wish-
ing you well! Shelley Lillie

THURSDAY, JUNE 12, 2008 8:39 AM, CDT

Erica and family,

We are so relieved that everything went well during surgery yester-
day. It is amazing what miracles occur on a daily basis. We send prayers
on this day of recovery.

Love, Elena, Brett, Sam, and Sophie MacDonald

THURSDAY, JUNE 12, 2008 9:14 AM, CDT

Todd,

Heard about the accident from Craig Hawley. So thankful that you are now in the recovery mode! Praying for your full recovery, guy. We miss you at QSP.

Jim Garrison

THURSDAY, JUNE 12, 2008 10:01 AM, CDT

Dear Todd and family,

I heard about your accident from our fellow SJU friend, Tom Ramboldt. I just wanted to send you a few extra words of encouragement! Keep fighting, and the pain will eventually go away. I work with Regions Hospital a little with my job at Boston Scientific, and it is a great hospital to be at when dealing with your types of injuries. They will take good care of you. Keep your eye on the long-term outcome and, with your determination, you will make a good recovery.

Best of luck! Paul Kahlert

THURSDAY, JUNE 12, 2008 10:14 AM, CDT

Fultz family,

Tracy just told me about the accident and I am so glad to hear that you are on the road to recovery. Remember that the Lord doesn't give us anything to handle without being with us through it all. Paul and I will keep you in our prayers and you know that we are here for you for anything that we can do to help.

We love you, Carol and Paul Carlson

THURSDAY, JUNE 12, 2008 10:40 AM, CDT

Todd and family,
We are praying for you and your family!
Kristi Beck

THURSDAY, JUNE 12, 2008 11:35 AM, CDT

We are just catching up on this incredible story of crisis, courage, and faith. Thank you for including us.

Our prayers are with you as family and friends surround Todd with faith, hope, and love . . . and the greatest of these is love.

May the love of Christ Jesus also abide with you for healing and peace.

In good faith, David and Muffy Tiede

THURSDAY, JUNE 12, 2008 3:19 PM, CDT

Todd and family,

Wish you the best toward a speedy recovery. If I can help in any way do not hesitate to contact me. All our prayers are with you and your family. Good Luck! Dave Galleberg and family

THURSDAY, JUNE 12, 2008 4:35 PM, CDT

Our thoughts and prayers are with your entire family.

Danielle Kressin

THURSDAY, JUNE 12, 2008 10:53 PM, CDT

Fultz family,

We just heard about the accident from some friends connected to a prayer chain. We thank God that Todd is still here to battle his injuries.

I am an old friend and neighbor of Todd's from New Prague. It's shocking and sad to hear about an old friend this way.

Please know that your whole family is in our thoughts and we pray for a full recovery for Todd. Based on the journal entries by friends and family, it sounds like Todd still has the same energy and fire that he had way back in the day.

Thank you for your updates on his condition. We will continue to check it for new updates on his recovery.

Brian and Margaret Bartyzal family

Glad to hear yesterday's surgery was successful. It sounds like Todd is really cooperating! I continue to pray for him and the rest of you through these long, long days.

Nancy Crothers

Dear Erica,

I was so shocked to hear of this horrific accident but so happy that Todd actually survived, especially after seeing those photos. You are a strong woman and having you by his side will get him through it. My best wishes go out to him always. Stay strong and my prayers are with you all.

Love, Allison Bahr

Todd, Erica, and family,

We are so happy to hear the good news about Todd's surgery. Keep fighting Fultzy! You and your family are in our daily thoughts and prayers.

Dan and Kim (Scheidt) Brown and family

Todd and family,

Great to hear the surgery was a success, and wish you the best in your recovery. I know your drive to succeed will get through these challenges. You will remain in our thoughts and prayers. Please let us know if there is anything we can do.

Will, Lottie, Willie, and Greta Steinke

To the Fultz family,

Our prayers are with your whole family. Glad to hear things are *progressing well, and even though it may be a long road ahead, we all know Fultzy is the ultimate fighter and will persevere. Once again, best wishes and we will keep you in our prayers daily.*

Andy, Libby, Tommy, and Katie Auger

THURSDAY, JUNE 12, 2008 8:47 AM, CDT

Todd,

You and your family are in my thoughts and prayers.

Shawn Vento

THURSDAY, JUNE 12, 2008 9:12 AM, CDT

Dear Todd and family,

Our thoughts and prayers have been with you during this last week. We are so happy the surgery went well yesterday. We hope all goes well with the rest of your recovery. Please, if we can do anything to help out we are here for you.

Our love, Kathy and Merv Salo

THURSDAY, JUNE 12, 2008 9:40 AM, CDT

Good morning Todd,

We've not met, but I am a pastor at Arlington Hills Lutheran Church, and I met your parents at a mutual friend's home a couple of weeks ago. They were telling my wife and me about the partnership program we have in Tanzania.

At any rate, when I learned of your accident, I stopped by after worship last Sunday and offered a brief prayer. As your folks were not there at the time, I did not disturb you to introduce myself. We will continue to hold you in prayer here at the church during this time of hospital care and recovery. May you know the healing touch of Jesus, and may His spirit be with you and your medical team.

Pastor Roger Allmendinger

THURSDAY, JUNE 12, 2008 9:43 AM, CDT

Dear Todd, Erica, and family,

I was so sorry to hear of Todd's accident but know that the prayers are coming in strong. I pray for a quick recovery and sleep for you, Erica! I know that this could be a long process but I will continue to keep you in my prayers.

Love, Jaci Wright

THURSDAY, JUNE 12, 2008 2:16 PM, CDT

To the entire Fultz family,

Just wanted to let you know that a lot of people are thinking of you guys from your "old stomping grounds" (New Prague). Todd is about as tough as they come. We are sending our thoughts and prayers your way!

Heather (Winn), Dennis, Tucker, Macy, and Reven Tietz

THURSDAY, JUNE 12, 2008 3:52 PM, CDT

Todd and family,

We are sending our best wishes and our prayers for a complete recovery for you. It sounds as if it will not be as quick or speedy as you would like: it probably never is, but getting better is what matters. It's been a very long time since we have seen you, but we remember a very caring and energetic person, and know that will help in your journey back to health. You and your family, as well as the Rebecks, whom we also know, are all in our prayers.

God bless, Dave and Kathy Okeson

THURSDAY, JUNE 12, 2008 4:06 PM, CDT

Hi Todd,

I just heard the news today and wanted to send along a note of support. I hope all goes well for you and your family. You've got great strength and a great God looking over you! Many prayers on your recovery. *(Thanks Erica for all the updates!)*

Take care, Kelley Stromberg Walhof

THURSDAY, JUNE 12, 2008 8:52 PM, CDT

Dear Todd, Erica and kids,

We are praying and cheering for you from Grand Rapids! Keep those miracles coming! We know God will grant you strength and patience in your recovery. We hope to see your famous smile soon.

Love and hugs to you all,

Cousin Karin, Todd, Erika, and Lindsay Cortese

FRIDAY, JUNE 13, 2008 8:31 AM, CDT

Fultzy,

I heard about your terrible accident and want you to know that you are in my family's prayers. Your list of friends is endless, so know that you have many, many people thinking about you and your family during this difficult time. Hang in there buddy.

John Lahti

THURSDAY, JUNE 12, 2008 11:24 PM, CDT

Fultzy,

We are thinking of you and wish you best! I am happy to hear that your surgeries have gone well and you are improving. I was working at the FLPD when I heard the accident come out over the radio. Though I love what I do, my worst nightmare is that a family member or a friend is involved. Keep fighting!

We will be thinking of you every day and keeping you and your family in our thoughts and prayers. Thank you to Erica and the entire Fultz family for keeping us updated on Todd's progress.

Rick and Colleen Peterson

FRIDAY, JUNE 13, 2008 9:00 AM, CDT

Todd,

We were so glad to hear the initial surgery went well, but know you will have a battle ahead of you as the doctors continue to do God's works of healing and mending. May God grant you peace and relief from the pain of healing in the hours and days to come.

Linda and I will continue to lift you up to God in our prayers.

Bob and Linda Rygh

FRIDAY, JUNE 13, 2008 10:24 AM, CDT

I am sorry to hear about your accident. My hopes and prayers are with you for a speedy recovery!

Dave Arndt

FRIDAY, JUNE 13, 2008 10:36 AM, CDT

Todd and family,

We just heard about your accident and wanted you to know our thoughts and prayers are with you and your family during this challenging time.

Jeff and Kelli Olson

FRIDAY, JUNE 13, 2008 1:02 PM, CDT

Erica,

I'm so happy to hear that Todd is improving every day. You both are so strong and driven—if anyone can pull through this you two can. I love the updates, keep them coming. Hang in there lady!

Mindy Gray

FRIDAY, JUNE 13, 2008 4:15 PM, CDT

Sorry to hear about your accident. Our thoughts and prayers are with you. Just remember, as mum would say, "Force yourself!"

Love to you all!

Natasha John and Matthew Tierney

FRIDAY, JUNE 13, 2008 7:00 PM, CDT

Hey Todd and Erica,

It is so great to hear you are doing so well but don't push yourself too hard! Robert says remember deer hunting is only a few months away and Clay and Cayla couldn't do it without you and your camera. Lord knows you are the only one who can walk forever and not break a sweat.

We are truly praying for a speedy recovery and hopefully fairly painless (and that you can get good meds). If there is anything we can do from this far away, Erica please give us a call, and also give Todd a big hug and kiss from me and tell him he is a real miracle.

Donna and Robert Caron

FRIDAY, JUNE 13, 2008 9:22 PM, CDT

Todd, My thoughts and prayers are with you and your family.

Doc (John Dockendorf)

FRIDAY, JUNE 13, 2008 10:05 PM, CDT

Hi Todd and family,

This is an old high school classmate/friend. You and your family are in our thoughts and prayers. I pray for God's peace and healing to continue in your speedy recovery. We will have some juice with you tonight as well.

Doesn't this remind us of all the little things we usually take for granted that are blessings and important? Todd, you are a blessing to all.

Tracy Hestekin-Christenson

Todd and family,

This is another old friend from high school. I do believe in miracles big and small. I have experienced them myself during a long journey of watching my daughter battle cancer. I know that prayers have amazing power, so I will do my part and pray for your recovery, strength, and health. I also know that angels do carry us on their wings.

God's peace,
Jacqui (Zank) Sufka

Fultzy, We just heard the news. Wow! It sounds like you have come a long way in the last couple of weeks. You are a warrior and we know you will rebound stronger than ever. Have a Happy Father's Day tomorrow, and know you are in our prayers!

Scott and Stacey Millett

Todd and family,

We have been getting updates from Jeff Boyle every day. We were so sorry to hear of your accident and pray for a speedy recovery. I know we will see you on the Edgecumbe court soon and joining us for a bucket at O'Gara's. Keep fighting and get well soon.

Greg Meyer

Greetings to all of you Fultz folks.

We are following Todd's progress with prayers and cheers. We pray that you all will have the patience and courage you need as you travel this unknown path toward wellness again.

Todd, we haven't seen you since our trip to Holden and your stay with us in Idaho Falls (many years ago) and we have never met your wife and children. But we know about you all through your mom and dad, and we care deeply about how you are doing. May God's blessings be heaped upon you all.

Paul and Kay Hanson

SUNDAY, JUNE 15, 2008 11:38 AM, CDT

Todd and Erica,

We heard from Coley McDonough and thought to check out CaringBridge and found you guys. Our thoughts and prayers are with you. We know how determined Todd is! He is an amazing person . . . just keep setting those goals.

All our best,

Nate (Rert) and Sarah Brown family (SJU 91)

SUNDAY, JUNE 15, 2008 8:43 PM, CDT

Please know you and your family have been in our thoughts and prayers since we heard about the accident. We will continue to pray for Todd's healing and recovery.

Emily and Mike Schug

MONDAY, JUNE 16, 2008 7:42 AM, CDT

Fultzes,

I love you all VERY much and I am praying for you all! I wish I could be there to help you out in any way possible but I am a bit outta reach, being halfway 'round the world. I hope to see you all when I return from Singapore in August. Love you all!

Kisses, Baby Jenna (Jenna Holm)

We were shocked to hear the news of your accident, Todd. Just letting you know that you and your entire family are in our thoughts and prayers here in Ireland and we wish you a speedy recovery.

All our love,

Katrina and Michael Seeley and Oisin McCaughley

Fultzy,

I just heard of your accident and have been catching up with your wife's journal entries. Wow! You're Superman to have survived. I can't imagine what you've been through and the work ahead of you to get well. My prayers are for you get through this as quickly and as easily as possible. God bless!

P.S. I still remember the best pass ever!

Grundy (Mark Grundhofer)

Hey Todd,

You are amazing! Keep on fighting like you are and I have no doubt that you'll be having a pint at O'Gara's on SPD. Blessings to you and your beautiful family.

Joanna (Leach Boyle) Eversman

Dear Todd and family,

I am sure you don't remember me all that well Todd, but we used to play together when your father was a pastor in New Prague. I heard of your accident through a mutual friend. I had no idea that we've been living only a few blocks from each other for quite some time.

I spoke with your parents last week just before having to go out of *town for a week. My family has been praying for you and we all wish you a very speedy recovery.*

Steve Parry and family

Fultzy,

Hey buddy, sorry to hear of your accident. I am glad that you are fighting to live. You have always been up to challenges, however this is a different type of challenge than you are used to. Erica, thank you for the updates—we all appreciate them! Take care and God bless. You have been in our prayers and will continue to be so. We will see you sometime soon.

Your friend,

Bryan Allen

Hey Todd,

Pretty incredible story. Keep fighting so some day you can make your triumphant return to the court at the FL alumni basketball tourney. You can even play with us old guys! Take care and our prayers are with you.

David Drolson

Todd,

You probably don't remember me, but our parents were acquainted through Marriage Encounter and we played together as kids when they got together (my parents are Gary and JoAnn Rivers).

We want you to know that you are in our prayers each day. Erica, we've not met, but I know who you are through Trinity. Your love of Todd and of the Lord shines through in your journal updates. Stay strong and know that there are many more people out there praying for your family.

Roberta Ehret (known back then as Bobbi)

TUESDAY, JUNE 17, 2008 9:03 PM, CDT

Hi Todd,

It has been a long time since I have seen or talked to you. I have heard about your accident from several people in New Prague. I have been watching your progress, and it is great to see you getting better. Take care, our prayers are with you.

Dan Pint

WEDNESDAY, JUNE 18, 2008 8:42 AM, CDT

Erica and Todd,

I heard about the accident as we were leaving for Florida. We prayed for you from Disney World! We will pray for you from Stillwater, too. Keep up the great work. We'd love to have the kids over to play sometime. If you need anything let us know.

Jacque Johnson

WEDNESDAY, JUNE 18, 2008 12:55 PM, CDT

I am keeping you in my thoughts and prayers and hoping you have a quick recovery.

Colleen Robinson

THURSDAY, JUNE 19, 2008 8:59 AM, CDT

Erica and Todd,

Thanks for keeping everyone so up-to-date. You will be in my thoughts tomorrow, as you are each day. Let me know what I can do . . . at the same number Todd set up for me years ago.

Amber Walsh

Hi Todd and Erica,

This is the first chance that I have gotten to visit your CaringBridge site. Erica, you are doing a great job keeping everyone updated. (I have been getting updates from friends before this.)

Todd, you look great. Keep the strong spirit alive. I just wanted to let you know that my family and I are keeping you all in our thoughts and prayers. If there is anything that you need, please let me know. (I know that Hearts at Home will be organizing help for you as you need it!) You can count on our support. Todd, we will be thinking of you, and praying for a successful surgery tomorrow. Peace and love,

Jill and Scott and family (The Kneeskerns)

Todd,

Just wanting you to know the prayer team at Holy Trinity Lutheran Church in Sidney has you in our prayers.

Betty Sauder

Todd,

It is so awesome to see you smiling after everything you've been through and everything you have in front of you. Know that I have been following your progress and praying for your recovery since I found out about the accident. Your strong faith and strong will, along with all the support that you are receiving, will surely make an incredible difference in your recovery. You have an incredible support team around you, Erica and the kids.

God bless all of you!

Kris Retica

I know God is being overwhelmed with prayers for you, Todd. May He be with you and your family tomorrow.

Thanks Erica for the updates. It is heartening to see him smiling. God bless you.

Trudy Klassen

Todd, You may not remember me, but I am a sister to Sandy Fultz, and we have met some of the times you've been down in the Tracy area. Just wanted you to know that we are following your progress, and we are all pulling for you, especially tomorrow before/during/after surgery. Best wishes for continued healing and strength to you and your whole family.

Darcy and Mike Carlson

Todd and Erica,

It was great to see your picture this week. The last time I saw you Todd, you were in so much pain! Sulli and I were out fishing yesterday and we told some good stories about you Todd. Of course Sulli and I broke a few things in the boat. Oh well. I will keep up the prayers for a fast recovery.

Thanks for the updates Erica, and good luck on Friday, Todd.

Zap (Todd Zapzalka)

Hi Todd, Erica, and family,

Erica you are a wonderful journal updater! It's so crazy when everyone wants to know what's going on and we all want to call and know everything. You are doing a wonderful job keeping us informed.

Todd you are incredible and strong! Keep up your positive attitude.

You know a good friend of mine told me once to "let God." He will take care of you and your family. He has been with you and will continue to be with you and your surgeons and your rehab staff. Your positive attitude is helping you so much more than you could possibly imagine!

I cried when I read what you said you saw in Tami's, your Mom's, and Erica's eyes. Fight, Todd, fight! You have so much to fight for! Praying for you and your family and a speedy recovery. Gotta get you out of that hospital and into the fresh summer air.

Love to you and your family. We New Praguers have been talking and e-mailing about you. I even forwarded to a friend of mine whose husband played football with you at St. John's, Mike Ramler. Mike is married to my friend Cindy (Wolf) Ramler.

Take care and God bless you!

Love, Jill Hines Roiger

THURSDAY, JUNE 19, 2008 11:17 AM, CDT

Todd and family,

I just wanted to say hi and let you know that my family and I will be keeping you all in our prayers. I am sorry to hear about the accident. Good luck tomorrow! We will pray for the surgeons as well. Keep up the efforts on getting better.

Kim (Rud) Nelson (and family)

THURSDAY, JUNE 19, 2008 11:19 AM, CDT

Todd, After seeing the photos of the vehicle, I have to admit I was a bit scared to read more. I am so glad to hear that your recovery has started and you have accepted the challenge, which will surprise no one. You are in our thoughts and prayers as you prepare for your surgery. We hope that everything goes as planned and good reports will continue. May God bless you through your recovery.

David Dolan

Hi Todd and Erica,

You haven't met us (yet), but we're friends of Don and Eunice, both in Minnesota and Tanzania. We've been following your CaringBridge entries, and you have been in our prayers and will continue to be. May God be with you both during this time of medical emergency.

Dorothy and Doug Chapman

Hi Todd and Erica,

We've been gone the last two weeks, so this is the first chance I've had to send a message. We're so glad to hear your recovery is going well and we will be thinking about you during your surgery tomorrow. We'll keep checking for updates and will be praying for your recovery to continue to be positive. Be well soon. Pete is looking forward to getting back to the man cave ASAP. Be strong, take care, and God bless,

Pete and Denise Cote

Good to see your winning smile Todd! Keep up the great healing! Have you started a wiffleball league yet for the patients and staff there on your floor?

See you soon,

Tom Hallberg

Todd and family,

I just received the link to your CaringBridge site. I have read your journal and all the incredible messages from your friends and family. It is apparent you have touched many people. You and your family are in my prayers.

Julie (Parry) Friese and family

THURSDAY, JUNE 19, 2008 9:08 PM, CDT

Todd and Erica,

Sending our best wishes your way for a successful surgery tomorrow and a quick recovery to follow. You certainly have the power of prayer on your side! It sounds like you have a wonderful outlook and attitude Todd. That will serve you well during your recovery. And Erica, you are amazingly strong. Your posts are always so positive and encouraging, even to those of us not in the middle of such a traumatic life event. Your family and your story is the reason we all hug our loved ones a little tighter when they leave us. God bless you all, tomorrow especially.

Carrie, Andy, Jack, and Charlie Sandquist

THURSDAY, JUNE 19, 2008 11:27 PM, CDT

Todd,

I just heard about this. Good luck tomorrow. We'll be praying for you.

Odie (Pete and Sarah Odegard)

FRIDAY, JUNE 20, 2008 9:03 AM, CDT

Hey Todd,

We have been keeping up on you via Rachel and this website. You have been in our prayers, and we will keep thinking about you. We are so impressed with your strength and positivity throughout this experience. We'd love to help out with you, Erica, and your kids in any way we can.

Love,

Leah, Pete, Ella, and Oren Hamilton

FRIDAY, JUNE 20, 2008 9:28 AM, CDT

Hey Fultzy,

It was great to see you the other day. I am pretty sure you will remember us being there this time. It was great seeing you back to yourself and in such great spirits.

I hope Walter's book helped you sleep last night! I know I slept just thinking about it. Good luck with the surgery today, and we will see you next week for a game of Intellivision football and maybe some horse racing.

Mick, Jodi, and Teagan Ramboldt

FRIDAY, JUNE 20, 2008 10:02 AM, CDT

Our family will be thinking about you today Todd, and praying for your speedy recovery.

The Olejniks

FRIDAY, JUNE 20, 2008 10:07 AM, CDT

Hi Todd,

I just heard last night about your crash. Strangely enough I was playing catcher for my son's baseball practice. I thought it was quite ironic that I would hear about you while playing baseball. (My son still can't believe that I took a college class about baseball!) My thoughts and prayers are with you and your family. Take care of yourself and I hope to see you soon. If I can track down Pooh Richardson, Dominique Wilkins, and Spud Webb, they will be there for the party when you come home.

Beth (Pearson) Peterson

FRIDAY, JUNE 20, 2008 11:26 AM, CDT

Todd, Sorry to hear of your accident. Best wishes on a quick and full recovery. Please know that you and your doctors will be in our family prayers.

Kyle Kirsch

Todd, It's great to see a picture of you smiling. You look so good, it's hard to believe everything you've been through. What an accomplishment! We hope your surgery goes smoothly and you can continue your recovery and rehab. You are a strong person: I never knew how much so until now. You and your family are in our thoughts and prayers daily. We are here if there is anything you guys need. Take care of yourself. There is obviously so much more you need to do in this lifetime! We'll save some ribs for you.

The Quaderers

Todd, All of us at Roof Depot have you and your family in our prayers. We hope that you have a speedy recovery. We miss your daily visits and conversations and hopefully you will be back at home soon. Get well and hope to see you soon.

Bob Thompson, Matt, Joel, Morgan, Dave, Victor, Steve, Chad, Chris

Todd, Glad to hear you are doing better. We've been thinking about you constantly. Hope to enjoy a bit of craic and a few fags (not!) with you when you get home! Erica, sounds like you are a very strong individual. Keep up the great work.

Best wishes and thoughts, Jim and Lisa Stahl

Dear Todd and Erica,

I have a story that I thought you might be interested in hearing. I was talking to my parents in New Richmond about the terrible accident that you were in. I told them that I had just met you. They knew about the accident, and said they also knew you. As we put things together, we found out that they actually did not know you, but rather the Rebecks. My dad (Vern Loehr) used to work for Ron. So we're out here saying our prayers for you and Ron, hoping for a recovery. I heard the sad news about Ron today, just after his coming to. Keep your head up Todd. It seems there are a lot of people in many places praying for you. With the way things are going, that should be a reminder to all of us to do a lot more praying! Erica, I'm proud of you. You're keeping strong, and that's the right thing to do now. I don't know where you find the strength, but it's moving mountains!

All the best to you both and your family,
Todd Loehr

Hey Todd,
Sorry to hear about your accident. Get well soon!
Your old teammate,
John Wakeman

Baoooooouuuuuuu, Fultzy,

It was great to hear from you last week. Get your rest because we have a lot of fishing to catch up on. I'll see you soon.

Duper (Brent DuPont)
P.S. You look better than Grandpa and Greg in the picture!

SUNDAY, JUNE 22, 2008 9:23 PM, CDT

Hey Fultzy,

Sorry to hear about your accident. Sounds like you are recovering pretty quickly. Keep it up. Look forward to seeing you this fall at an SJU football game, if not sooner. God bless. My thoughts and prayers are with you. Stay strong.

Bif (Jim Bifaro)

SUNDAY, JUNE 22, 2008 10:24 PM, CDT

Todd,

Just heard today about your accident. We are so glad to hear that things are improving! You are in our thoughts and prayers.

Take care and God bless,

Steve and Jill O'Toole

MONDAY, JUNE 23, 2008 3:20 PM, CDT

Hey Fultzy,

I just heard about your accident. I'm glad to see you are making a comeback! My thoughts and prayers are with you buddy. Remember when you ran track your senior year and we always dreaded the John Lautigar 400-meter intervals. Throwing up and having do to it over and over again! Keep fighting . . .Get well and hope to see you soon,

Chris Kauls

MONDAY, JUNE 23, 2008 11:26 AM, CDT

Todd,

God bless and stay strong. All of the McDonoughs are thinking of you and praying for you.

Jim McDonough

Todd,

I really don't understand why things like this happen to people. I believe your strength and drive with get you through this and you will be out fishing with your kids soon. If there is anything I can do to help you or your family please let me know. Our golf event will be fine but we will miss you. I will bring you some new shirts after everything settles down. We will continue to pray for a quick recovery. Have a great day.

Paul Broten

Hi Todd,

Mrs. Hallberg told me you were doing well when I was home last weekend visiting my Mom. You look like you are healing well. You are in my thoughts and prayers.

Love, Amy Schumacher

Dear Todd,

My wife, Mary Ann, and I are longtime friends of your parents. In fact, our ties reach back to our college years at Gustavus! Our ties are also strong through the ELCA in which I am a pastor. We were out of town and did not hear of your car accident and injuries until last Sunday when we saw that you were on the prayer list at Incarnation. Your mom and dad e-mailed us about the situation and directed us to Caring Bridge. As you know, you have been surrounded by hundreds, no thousands, of praying people. We are among them. We are heartened by the news of your good progress and pray that the Spirit of God and all the loving, skilled hands that have upheld and cared for you will continue to give you strength and healing.

Gary and Mary Ann Anderson

WEDNESDAY, JUNE 25, 2008 7:46 AM, CDT

Todd and Erica,

I'm a friend of Erica's from Hearts of the Home moms. I've been reading your updates daily and keeping you and your family in prayer and thought. You've both demonstrated strength and continue to move forward. Here's a verse for you both: "The people who know their God will display strength and take action." Daniel 11:32

Blessings to you both, Nancy Robertson

WEDNESDAY, JUNE 25, 2008 1:15 PM, CDT

Todd and Erica,

It is so great to see your progress! Thanks for letting Erica sneak away on Saturday night. I think the Girl's Night Out was just what she needed. Even though I am far away, let me know what I can do when you get home. Hope to see more of these great photos.

Lots of love, Patrice Bailey

WEDNESDAY, JUNE 25, 2008 1:43 PM, CDT

Looking good Fultzy! Talk to you soon.

Kman (Andy Klassen)

WEDNESDAY, JUNE 25, 2008 3:32 PM, CDT

Erica,

That is so great to hear! Please let us know what we can do to help out. We enjoy reading your updates and so impressed with Todd's recovery!

Dale and Jessica Schuldt

WEDNESDAY, JUNE 25, 2008 10:46 PM, CDT

Hello, Todd and Erica,

Just a note from a fellow Johnnie: a really old one. I'm so old, Todd, that I remember having your parents in my first English classes in Wal-

nut Grove. I left SJU in '52 close to when Professor Gagliardi came to campus. Claire and I are well aware of how "interesting" your lives have become and we think of you each day. Sounds as though you are in good hands. It's great to follow your progress, Todd, thanks to Erica, and we will continue to do so.

> *Blessings to you both,*
> *Gene and Claire Fox*

THURSDAY, JUNE 26, 2008 6:57 AM, CDT

> *Todd,*
> *Glad to see that your recovery is going great!*
> *Ed Friesen*

THURSDAY, JUNE 26, 2008 10:48 AM, CDT

> *Holy crap! I spoke to Doug Ekvall a couple of days ago who let me know your current condition.*
> *Frankly, I found your photo a little disturbing as I thought you were trying to show us what is under the gown. Thank goodness I did not look at the expanded version!*
> *At any rate, it looks like you are progressing at a breakneck (pun intended) speed, which is about what I would expect from you. Hope to see you around the rink soon!*
> *Murph and the two little murphs (Mike Murphy)*

THURSDAY, JUNE 26, 2008 6:51 PM, CDT

> *Hi Todd,*
> *Phil and I are thinking of you all the time. It sounds like you're doing really well.*
> *Did Erica tell you that we were there your first day? You were unconscious. Keep up the good work. I hope you'll be home soon.*
> *Much love, Debbie and Phil Peterson*

Todd,

Today Erica, I, and a crew of helpers worked to make your home-coming a comfortable one. Since you mischievously surprised me yesterday—sneaking up on me in your wheelchair while I looked for you in your bed—it is clear that you are ready to bust out of there!

I know you worked hard all day today practicing your in-and-out of bed skills so you can manage the transition on Saturday. Erica is thinking through all the details. She sure does love you! The kids will no doubt be driven silly with enthusiasm to have their wonderful daddy home again.

Today we moved the den furniture to accommodate your bed, went to Target and bought what you might need, and talked with the construction crew about the ramp that will be ready for you by Saturday. Tomorrow the door will be widened. All that is left is your arrival home!

I am very proud of you and all you have endured these last three weeks. I am so grateful to have you back, and to have a chance to help you when you needed it most. Now, let the games begin . . . day one of the homecoming celebrations!

Love, Judi (Judith Savage)

Hey Todd,

Wonderful to hear that you are heading home. I'm sure having your family around will help you heal even faster.

Thanks Erica for the updates, you sound like a pretty amazing woman!

Jenne (Jewell) Nord

FRIDAY, JUNE 27, 2008 1:25 PM, CDT

Todd, It's so nice to see your smiling face and see how far you have come: your positive attitude makes a big difference!

Erica, Thanks for the updates. Let us know what we can do to help after everybody gets settled!

Love,

Chuck, Melissa, Nathan, and Allison Alshouse

FRIDAY, JUNE 27, 2008 10:55 PM, CDT

Todd,

I was out with some college girls last night and heard of your accident. I am glad to have read on the site about you coming home tomorrow. That is such wonderful news. There is no place like home. Your recovery will be so much more comforting.

You are in my thoughts and prayers. Continue to keep your strong will and determination throughout your recovery.

God bless and take care,

Tammy Supan

SATURDAY, JUNE 28, 2008 4:59 PM, CDT

Todd,

Great to hear you're at home! We continue to think of you and pray for your continued improvement.

John Simonsen

SATURDAY, JUNE 28, 2008 10:44 PM, CDT

Todd,

It is so good to hear that you are home. We have been praying for you and will continue to pray for your complete recovery. Thanks for your CaringBridge communication.

Love, Judy and Leroy Olheiser

Erica,

I am so happy for you that your Todd is back home with you and the kids. He looks so happy in the picture! All our prayers have been answered. Will continue to pray for you and Todd. Also will be keeping Karl in our prayers.

Jo Ann Dworshak

Todd,

Like others have said, it is so great to see the picture of you in the van coming home and your big smile! My family has followed your recovery and we have kept you and your family in our thoughts and prayers. What tremendous progress you have made! Keep up the hard work with your rehab—we are pulling for you to make a full recovery. If anyone can do it, you can.

Amy Gross

Our thoughts and prayers are with you all. Your recovery story has been amazing!

Carrie and Luke Scardigli

Todd,

Heard of your accident and wanted to let you know we are thinking of you and your family. Glad to see you making a strong recovery!

Willie and Jill Seiler

THURSDAY, JULY 3, 2008 3:27 AM, CDT

Todd,

Just saw the article in the Times, and I am so glad that you are going to have a great recovery. I knew you from high school and I had no idea about the accident! Sounds like everything is on the up and up and I hope it continues that way. Hope the best for you and your family!

Take care, Tony Megahan

SUNDAY, JULY 6, 2008 5:34 PM, CDT

Hey Fultzy,

I heard about your accident through my brother and dad. I am glad to hear that you are making such good progress. You and your family are in our thoughts and prayers. I am glad that you are finally home and reunited with your family.

Good luck and best wishes for a speedy recovery. I hope you and your family had a wonderful 4th of July!

Take care Fultzy!

Pam (Sonntag) Nelson

TUESDAY, JULY 8, 2008 5:04 PM, CDT

Todd and Erica,

So glad to hear Todd is doing so well. You are such a fighter, Todd! Keep up the good work.

Erica, you are amazing! Your spirit and faith throughout this ordeal has been so uplifting to me.

Gary and I know Don and Eunice. I have been keeping current on Todd's progress and he has been in my prayers. Your faith tells the healing story for all.

God's blessings,

Sharon and Gary Moody

Todd, Erica, and family,

How wonderful to see your own message today, Todd! We continue to hold all of you in our hearts and pray that each day brings those little victories you speak of! We pray for healing, patience, and a sense of humor! Keep up the great work!

Brian and Jennifer Tolzmann

Hi Todd,

Just found out about your accident. Only a strong person like yourself could survive everything you've gone through. I think back to your football days at SJU and all the victories you contributed to. Now you have one more victory to accomplish and I know you will win again. Our prayers, thoughts, and good wishes are with you and your family. We will try to make it to your benefit. Look forward to seeing you soon.

Tom Arth

Very glad to hear of your progress. Remember, keep squeezing your trigger finger and squinting with your left eye. Per Winston Churchill, "Nevaaah give up!"

George Winn

Todd, Erica, and family,

I just learned of the accident. Please know you are all in my thoughts and prayers. I know the road that you have taken and the road you have ahead of you. I also know how strong you are Todd. You will overcome this and come out the other side an even stronger person!

I am so impressed with your progress thus far. I know it takes a lot of faith and love to get to where you are now so quickly. I wish you and your family only the very best. I am sorry I will not be able to join you all at the benefit. Please know I will be thinking of you on 08-08-08 especially. I will keep checking up on you to see how you are doing. Good thoughts and prayers from out west!

Melissa Plummer

SUNDAY, JULY 20, 2008 8:37 PM, CDT

Todd and all,

We are keeping close track of your progress from out here in Michigan. It seems to be going well, otherwise I hope you know I would be driving over there to whip you into shape. (Yeah right, it looks like there are plenty of others to share that role.) Marc, Megan, Joe and I are all pulling for you and wonder every day what new things you and your family are going through.

We are sorry that we won't be able to be at the benefit, but Karin, Todd, and the kids will be out here so we will "tilt a glass in your honor" for sure. Please let us know if there is anything we can do for you.

Family is a special thing, and different than friendship. "You can pick your friends, but you're stuck with your family." I'm happy with my family, and hope you are, too!

Love, hugs, and best wishes,
Katie Setterlund

WEDNESDAY, JULY 23, 2008 3:53 PM, CDT

Hi Todd,

I'm one of those "Tanzania pastors" who know you through your parents. Great to hear of your steady progress and healing. Just read about "the classics" from the coach at St. John's—what wisdom he gave you for a time such as this. You are in my prayers.

Bonnie Wilcox

THURSDAY, JULY 24, 2008 3:26 PM, CDT

Hey Todd,

Was told a little about what happened to you from Andy Schultz a couple weeks ago. Don't know if you remember me: I'm from Columbia Heights, same year as you. We did a couple of basketball camps together (remember the time you formed a turd out of the brownie they gave us at Lakeside Basketball camp and put it on someone's pillow, then took a bite as he watched and freaked out?). Hope you don't mind the note, just wanted to wish you all the best, my thoughts and prayers are with you and your family. Sounds like you're on the road to recovery!

Dave Gerda

MONDAY, JULY 28, 2008 2:43 PM, CDT

Todd,

Just a quick note to let you know that you have been in our prayers on a regular basis. It looks to me like things are progressing quite nicely. Keep up the great work and know that you can count on the power of prayer. Our best to you!

God bless,

Tim and Jeanette Weisz

WEDNESDAY, AUGUST 6, 2008 2:06 PM, CDT

Hi Todd,

I hope that this message finds you well. Just wanted to let you know that I was thinking about you and hoping for your quick recovery. Be well!

Megan Reardon

THURSDAY, AUGUST 7, 2008 12:54 PM, CDT

Todd,

I just talked with Stacey Ehlers-Millett and heard about your accident. You and your family are in my thoughts and prayers. I hope and pray for your continued recovery.

Sarah Dineen (CSB 1992)

FRIDAY, AUGUST 8, 2008 7:16 AM, CDT

Wanted to let the whole Fultz gang know we wish were with you for the big gig tonight! You continue to be in our prayers which, given your progress, are already being answered.

Love,

Kersten and Charlie Larson

FRIDAY, AUGUST 8, 2008 11:50 AM, CDT

Todd and Erica,

We don't know each other, but my husband and I read the story in the Gazette, and wanted you to know that we are thinking and praying for a quick and full recovery. We relate to your story, as my husband was in a severe waterskiing accident five years ago.

We are touched by your story and the positive attitude that you both seem to have—it is a very important part of the healing process. We are planning on coming to the benefit tonight if it is open to the public.

Best wishes,

Jen and Greg Boner

Todd and family,

Just wanted to stop by and say hi and that I am thinking of you guys. I wish I could have made it to your party, I am sure it was wonderful. My prayers are with you!

Best Wishes,

Lindsey Buege

It is your old friend, Jona Turner (now Van Deun). I hope you are healing. I wish you good prayers and a speedy recovery: you are not the kind of person to sit still for very long. Please give my best to your family.

Jona Van Deun

Hi Todd and family,

I'm so excited for you! I've been faithfully following your story since the middle of June when Joyelle asked for prayers for you. I even bought and read Tiger Tim and loaned it to Joyelle!

In the middle of July the kids and I drove to Wisconsin and came back thru Minnesota and I so wanted to stop and meet you but we just didn't have enough time. Maybe next time. Glenda says I remind her of your mom: what an awesome compliment!

Well, I just wanted to let you know I pray for you regularly as does our Holy Trinity church family. May God continue to bless you with complete earthly healing as you are such a blessing to so many. Have an awesome day, week, and month: so much to look forward to! By the way, my niece, Rachel, works at Forest Lake Floral, so we've talked about you!

Joy in Jesus, Debra Bird

Hi Todd,

I'm so glad to hear that you are recovering well. Knowing you, you will be back to doing all the things you love to do. Nice pictures of your family and parents. Good to see them. I hope all continues to go well and we get a chance to catch up soon.

Love ya! Jody Waisanen

Way Fultzy!

Soon you will be back to your playing weight and forty times, light years ahead of the rest of us couch potatoes.

Mark Peller

Hello Todd,

I and my wife, Rene, are friends of your folks. Faith sponsored our family for a time while we were missionaries with the ELCA. We have not stayed in close contact these past years and have lost touch.

But today, while participating in a parade here in U.P. Michigan, a woman from the crowd came up to introduce herself to me. Her name is Jill Somrock. She and her husband are members of Faith.

She shared with us your story and the remarkable recovery you are making. Please greet Don and Eunice. We pray grace, courage, and humor for the journey ahead. Philip Johnson

Todd,

It's great to see you standing! Congratulations, you're truly an inspiration! Brenda (Gabrick) Brophy

SATURDAY, OCTOBER 25, 2008 10:30 AM, CDT

Hi Todd,

I have not signed your book lately but I read your entries every time they are updated. Your courage and strength is amazing. I am so happy for you and your family. You are in my prayers nightly and I look forward to your next entry. Keep up the good work and best of luck during your next fishing outing!

Lisa Lehtinen

TUESDAY, OCTOBER 28, 2008 12:37 PM, CDT

We are so happy to hear and read of your progress. You and your family have been in our thoughts and prayers.

I spoke to Pastor Don and Eunice yesterday and it was great to hear the joy in their voices as they spoke of your progress, of Erica and the kids, and (of course) the upcoming fishing trip. You are a true inspiration to many. Your courage, strength, and positive attitude is so amazing. Keep it up. Todd, we wish you and your family well and we're all praying for your speedy recovery.

Sally and Crispin Semakula

WEDNESDAY, NOVEMBER 12, 2008 8:15 PM, CST

Congratulations Todd, I'm so glad you are doing so well! Thinking about you!

God bless,

Gretchen Fritz

WEDNESDAY, NOVEMBER 12, 2008 9:57 PM, CST

Wanna race?

Frank Drebin

THURSDAY, NOVEMBER 13, 2008 8:59 AM, CST

I think everyone who has followed your journey has won! What a truly amazing man you are. Thank you so much for sharing. You made my day once again.

Stacy Hallberg and family

TUESDAY, NOVEMBER 18, 2008 1:53 PM, CST

Hello Todd,

I have been following your journey: congrats on walking! My husband is not a big computer user, so I have been providing him updates (Doug Ekvall, former Forest Lake classmate and cousin of Wendy Castellano). We have a three-year-old daughter and a four-year-old son. Your journey and inspirational messages have made me a better parent!

Keep walking,
Nancy Ekvall

WEDNESDAY, NOVEMBER 19, 2008 11:00 AM, CST

Congrats Todd! You look great in the picture. Amy and I check out the site frequently. What an inspiration. You guys have been in our thoughts and prayers.

Rick, Amy, Hailey, and Mackenzie Slachta

WEDNESDAY, JANUARY 14, 2009 6:37 AM, CST

Hi, Just me wishing you a speedy recovery. A friend is a person with whom you can be yourself and with whom you don't have to pretend. A friend is someone like you.

God bless you all,
Geraldine Seeley

THURSDAY, JANUARY 15, 2009 10:01 PM, CST

Just want you both to know that the Terweys are keeping you in our prayers all day, every day. Please don't hesitate to let us know if you need anything.

Todd, get well soon . . . I need you to get JT up to the fishhouse.

Love you all,

Jason and Lydia Newlin

FRIDAY, JANUARY 16, 2009 6:25 PM, CST

We wanted to let you know, Todd, that you and your family are and have been in our thoughts and prayers.

Jeff Windfeldt

SATURDAY, JANUARY 17, 2009 8:13 PM, CST

We are thinking of you. If you or Erica need anything let us know. I was up in Forest Lake at Faith today. I laughed as I looked over at the front pew and thought of all the times you slid in late (and at the fact that this story still makes us laugh). Hope you were able to watch some hockey today! Stay strong.

Suzy Lindeberg

SATURDAY, JANUARY 17, 2009 9.17 PM, CST

Dear Todd and family,

Just wanted to assure you that you are included in the daily prayers of our family.

God bless you, Brian and Rachel Bonin family

TUESDAY, JANUARY 20, 2009 10:21 PM, CST

Hi Todd,

I had no idea what you have been through the past year. While cruising an older issue of the Stillwater newspaper online I saw your name, which led to the article on the accident. It probably sounds cliché by now, but I will add you and your family to my daily thoughts and prayers. I will pray that you will be in gentle, knowledgeable hands as you recover and that your family will be comforted and supported as you heal and that God would be somehow glorified through your current suffering. Even with all that medical junk strapped on you, you are still smiling. Todd Fultz was always smiling.

Brian Solum

P.S. Nice deer.

THURSDAY, MAY 7, 2009 7:03 PM, CDT

Todd and family,

Congrats on your improvement and return home.

It has been years since I have seen you, but I recall the time at SJU like it was yesterday. You were full of life and energy then . . . and from reading this site, it is great to see that you still are!

Continue to be strong, you're in our prayers!

Don Savelkoul

SATURDAY, MAY 16, 2009 7:52 PM, CDT

Todd and Erica,

Wow . . . thank the Lord for your spirit and fight! You look great. I have thought and prayed for you and your family often. Just today in between coaching my daughters' basketball games, I asked my mother if she had heard any updates about you. (Your folks have visited their church, Christ the King in New Brighton, to talk about Africa and they share common friends.)

She hadn't heard and when we returned home, I picked up the mail and there was your victory party invitation with the CaringBridge link. My heart reaches out to you, to Erica and your family and the challenges this past year has brought you. I've been reading a few postings and it looks like you are changing and inspiring lives. Hold on to that, hold on to God, and use the spirit, strength, and faith God gave you to recover to your max!

Blessings,

Janel Moeller (Palyan)

MONDAY, JUNE 15, 2009 9:25 AM, CDT

Hi Todd,

Sorry we could not make your walking party, but sounds like it was an amazing night! I'm so thrilled for you and your family. You've worked so hard and deserve all the blessings God can throw your way.

Take care,

Jill (Wavrin) Grindahl

MONDAY, MAY 17, 2010 12:41 PM, CDT

Hi Todd,

I just happened to read the Pioneer Press from this weekend today and saw the story about you. You are one amazing and inspirational man. It has been a long time since we've seen you, since back in the day when I worked for you at Sal's Bar with Stacy back in college.

I wish you all the best as you continue your recovery. It looks like you have a wonderful family and many blessings.

God bless you,

Melanie (Larson) Willy

Hello Todd and family,

I am just today reading about what has happened in your life since I last spoke with you in 2000. I am happy to see that you have three wonderful children and continue to stand in the light. Your remarkable strength and trust in our Heavenly Father's love for you is an inspiration. Thank you so much for sharing your journey. I trust that your recovery continues and your pain has abated with the additional surgeries.

Best to you forever,

Lynn Peroceschi

Todd,

I haven't seen you for many years. (Governor's Mansion?) Before I read your article in Sunday's paper I knew nothing of the accident. What an amazing story! Your positive attitude and outlook on life is admirable. Best wishes as you continue your journey.

Take care,

Jill Pelke (Petkoff)